London never gets old to me; it's timeless. It might be seen as the land of afternoon tea-drinkers, nibbling on dainty sandwiches and scones, or the land of beer-drinkers enjoying the many pubs as soon as the working day ends, but while these clichés are true, there is so much more.

This city offers something to suit everyone, whether it be shopping galore, eating in restaurants that offer cuisines from all over the world, soaking up the history or relishing the brand new, wandering around contemporary art spaces, sampling the pubs and bars, scouring hip boutiques for vintage gems or relaxing in the green spaces that pepper the urban sprawl. There's a real energy wherever you [illegible] – and this guid[illegible]ic [illegible]

the hunt london writer

david leppan

David Leppan is a treasure hunter and a collector – a hunter-gatherer. His penchant for what's unique, rare and handmade was first piqued at the tender age of 10, when a friend's father told him with huge enthusiasm about his prize classic car. At the age of 20, in order to finance his rather nomadic student lifestyle, he started hunting: passionately buying and rather sadly selling antiques. Luckily, he's since started gathering instead. Today, he is a self-confessed addict of beautiful and unusual products made by craftsmen and artisans, as well as those made by their predecessors.

where to lay your weary head

Rest up, relax and recharge

THE PORTOBELLO HOTEL

HAZLITT'S

Eighteenth-century home turned characterful luxury hotel

6 Frith Street (W1D 3JA) / +44 (0)20 7434 1771 / hazlittshotel.com

Double from £187

"Travel's greatest purpose is to replace an empty mind with an open one." Or at least that's what essayist William Hazlitt reckoned. This four-story Georgian townhouse is where Hazlitt died in 1830. Now an upscale hotel, Hazlitt's pays homage to its namesake by welcoming an array of open-minded guests and wowing them with rooms that boast four-poster beds, claw-footed tubs, oil paintings and loads of lovely antiques.

THE CAPITAL HOTEL

Charming, family-run plush bolt-hole

22-24 Basil Street (SW3 1AT) / +44 (0)20 7591 1200 / capitalhotel.co.uk

Double from £245

This has been a hidden oasis for many, including myself, for years. For 40 years David Levin, and now his daughter, Kate, too, has owned and operated this little gem. David started his career as a commis waiter in 1952 and worked his way up to creating The Capital in 1971. When the bustle of Knightsbridge becomes just too much for me and I need to escape for a drink or lunch, this is a quiet, peaceful and friendly haven. It's also an ideal location for shopping or for business

THE FOX CLUB

A little Mayfair pad

46 Clarges Street (W1J 7ER) / +44 (0)20 7495 3656 / foxclublondon.com

Double from £200

Although this place is small, with only nine rooms, it's a wonderful place to stay. Handily placed next to busy Green Park station, The Fox Club is a retreat for relaxing not far from London's hustle and bustle. The hotel has a sleek design, in keeping with its title, with comfortable well-kept rooms that are stylish and cool but luxurious at the same time.

THE PORTOBELLO HOTEL

Boutique comfort in west London

22 Stanley Gardens (W11 2NG) / +44 (0)20 7727 2777 / portobellohotel.com

Double from £215

Superbly located, the stunning Portobello Hotel stands in the pretty area of Notting Hill. It's romantic and decadent in its décor, and it doesn't really feel like a hotel, but more like a home-away-from-home. It has a cozy cottage atmosphere, almost as if when you draw the curtains it seems like you're tucked away in the woods somewhere.

THE CAPITAL HOTEL

THE ROCKWELL

Comfortable, convenient and elegant accommodation

181-183 Cromwell Road (SW5 0SF) / +44 (0)20 7244 2000 / therockwell.com

Double from £100

A 40-room boutique hotel, The Rockwell sits smartly on Cromwell Road in Kensington, unfazed by the ceaseless traffic zipping along central London's main thoroughfare to Heathrow Airport. Double-glazed windows throughout the property and a splendid courtyard terrace in the back garden will do that for a place. Keep it in mind for easy access to transport, museums and parks. Inside, expect a traditional English feel tastefully accentuated with the most stylish of contemporary design accoutrements.

THE ZETTER TOWNHOUSE

Ornately multifarious digs for fashionable scenesters

49-50 St John's Square (EC1V 4JJ) / +44 (0)20 7324 4567
thezettertownhouse.com

Double from £160

Almost equidistant between Soho Square and Hoxton Square (a little more than a mile each way), this Georgian townhouse features a baker's dozen of stylishly eclectic rooms. The offshoot of the next door "quirky vintage-modern" Zetter Hotel, the Zetter Townhouse is the darling destination of journos and fashionistas. Even if you're not staying here, you'd be wise to drop by the much-lauded and rather lavish bar for a drink from a list mixed up by 69 Colebrooke Row's (pg 133) booze maestro Tony Conigliaro.

TOWN HALL HOTEL

Prime base for East End explorers

Patriot Square (E2 9NF) / +44 (0)20 7871 0460 / townhallhotel.com

Double from £173

This former 1910 council government building in Bethnal Green matches Edwardian elements and modern comforts with minimal clash. From its rooftop conservatory to its basement pool, with especially spacious rooms all individually designed and a couple of fine-dining hot spots in between, Town Hall Hotel serves as an ideal base for luxury digs when you're not out gallery hopping and pop-up plundering along this eastern frontier of Shoreditch.

THE ZETTER TOWNHOUSE

st james's and mayfair

In this exclusive hub of private clubs, royal academies and ultra rich residences, the shopping is haute, the dining scene exquisite and the nightlife vibrant. However you'd like to dispose of your discretionary income, you certainly can do it here (and you'd be wise to check the dress code before queuing up to get in anywhere). Even a cursory cruise through the smart streets of St James's and Mayfair reveals that Michelin stars, chauffeured cars and royal warrants are in abundance. Still, this exceptionally well-connected swath of central London is at the very least worth wandering around, even if you're on a tightly budgeted itinerary. Situated beside some of London's loveliest parks and home to its prettiest garden squares, most historic shops, world class galleries and famed thoroughfares, the area grants rare access to the goings-on of upper crust English society as well as a window to the daily affairs of the globally affluent.

1 Alfred Dunhill's Bourdon House Barber
2 Berry Bros & Rudd
3 Cecconi's
4 D.R. Harris & Co. Ltd
5 Drake's
6 Fortnum & Mason
7 G.J. Cleverley & Co.
8 Lock & Co. Hatters
9 Paxton & Whitfield
10 Peter Edwards
11 Philip Mould
12 Scotts
13 Smythson

ALFRED DUNHILL'S BOURDON HOUSE BARBER

Gentlemen's grooming

2 Davies Street (W1K 3DJ) / +44 (0)20 7853 4440
dunhill.co.uk/the-homes/london/#the_barber / Closed Sunday

Just off Berkeley Square, The Duke of Westminster's former home today houses not only Dunhill's flagship store in London but also their club, Alfred's. Within this splendid property the barbershop is a personal highlight, although I admit a drink in the courtyard garden is pretty high on my list, too. Jay, the resident barber is a traveler. Of South American descent, he lived in Singapore for years and now calls London home and as such you can talk to him about, well, anything (and in various languages). You'll be offered a cup of tea or coffee while your hair is cut or your beard trimmed, and any products used will be the old-school likes of D.R. Harris (pg 15). It's wonderful to escape to an oasis of yesteryear like this every so often.

BERRY BROS & RUDD

Cellars deep beneath St James's

3 St James Street (SW1A 1EG) / +44 (0)20 7022 8973 / bbr.com
Closed Sunday

This shop is British vintner history in bricks and mortar. For over 300 years this family-run business has supplied London with wine and, at its outset, with coffee. The giant scales used to weigh the coffee beans (still there to this day), were also used to weigh the well-heeled gentry back then. Since the days of King George III, these merchants have supplied the Royal Household and still carry two royal warrants (for Her Majesty The Queen and His Royal Highness Prince Charles), as well as being able to serve the likes of you and me with a highly impressive range of wines, ports and spirits. I once had cause to make apology to a Scottish lord, for a missed dinner, and a bottle of whisky from the very distillery closest to his home certainly helped. Berry Bros & Rudd came to my rescue.

CECCONI'S

Venetian hospitality

5A Burlington Gardens (W1S 3EP) / +44 (0)20 7434 1500
cecconis.co.uk / Open daily

Found by walking through the Burlington Arcade from Piccadilly, behind the Royal Academy of Arts, this Italian restaurant is always fun, at any time of day, any day of the week. Cecconi's brought a little bit of Italy to London back in 1978, and still the gorgeous, plush green chairs and the Venetian food allow you to escape the city for an hour or two, or more. You could actually stay here all day, as breakfast is served from 7am and they stay open until 1am. I love the chicken liver crostini with onion chutney, followed by the fresh buffalo ricotta ravioli. Or you can nibble on cicchetti, savor the delicate sea bass tartare, or tuck into beef tagliata with wild chicory.

D.R. HARRIS & CO. LTD

Toiletries for the gents

29 St James's Street (SW1Y 6AY) / +44 (0)20 7930 3915
drharris.co.uk / Closed Sunday

Only in recent times did I discover this old perfumery, but they've been in St James's since 1790. Started by a surgeon, Henry Harris and a chemist, Daniel Rotely (D.R.), the shop has long been used by the Royal family and the gentry of the area. It was Jay, my barber at Alfred Dunhill's Bourdon House (pg 12), who first used their Crystal hair cream on me (described as a "fixative – no oil or grease") and I must say I go nowhere without it now. This is a splendid shop with loads of practical things once found in traditional pharmacies on every high street.

DRAKE'S

Handmade ties of distinction

3 Clifford Street (W1S 2LF) / +44 (0)20 7734 2367
drakes-london.com / Closed Sunday

I used to find it a challenge to track down quality menswear accessories that were nicely different from the standard, mass-produced items on the high street. That is, until I came across my first pocket square by Drake's. England's largest independent producer of handmade ties actually started out in 1977 as a provider of quality scarves, with an ethos that "true luxury is indeed the comprehension of quality". Still going strong today, they produce the most striking array of neckwear and even offer a bespoke tie range. They have extended their range to include clothing but I especially like their cufflinks and belts. My absolute favorite item is their shoe-horn made from Scottish stag antler and ox horn.

FORTNUM & MASON

Teas, preserves and hampers galore

181 Piccadilly (W1A 1ER) / +44 (0)20 7734 8040
fortnumandmason.com / Open daily

How does one go about describing an institution that's been around since the early 1700's and continues to supply the finest hampers in the land? Between Piccadilly and Jermyn Street, Fortnum's window displays always raise a smile. Whether it's during the Wimbledon Championship, Christmas or the Queen's Jubilee, Britishness is celebrated in its most glorious traditions here. The ground and lower ground floors are a grocery store par excellence, ideal for some picnic treats or souvenirs and gifts. There are two products that make my Christmas list every year: the Fortnum & Mason hampers – wicker baskets stuffed with all sorts of goodies including their teas, cakes and biscuits, or cheeses, pâtés and wines – and the honey from the beehives on the rooftop, overlooking St James's and Mayfair.

G.J. CLEVERLEY & CO.

A bespoke shoe institution

28 Old Bond Street (W1S 4SL) / +44 (0)20 7493 0443
gjcleverley.co.uk / Closed Sunday

In the midst of the hubbub of Mayfair, side-tracking off Bond Street into
the Royal Arcade, some things simply haven't changed for years. I love
that! Here, in the first floor workshop, you can still witness the making of
some of London's most exceptional shoes. The original George Cleverley
passed his business onto George Glasgow and John Carnera, who continue
taking on apprentices themselves, ensuring that the tradition that shoed
the feet of Winston Churchill, John Gielgud and Laurence Olivier, is still
thriving today. Don't forget to select a few brightly colored pairs of socks to
complement both of your individually made-to-measure shoes – yes, each
shoe made precisely to fit each foot, because "no-one has a pair of feet".

LOCK & CO. HATTERS

The world's oldest hat shop

6 St James Street (SW1A 1EF) / +44 (0)20 7930 8874
lockhatters.co.uk / Closed Sunday

No sooner do you discover one 300-year-old, family-run business around here, when another comes along. This is the UK, after all: everywhere you step is steeped in history. And this institution is endearingly representative of Britishness. Having provided headwear to the likes of Admiral Lord Nelson (he of Trafalgar Square) and Charlie Chaplin, this is the oldest hat shop in the world. It's quite something to think that it was established when the West End was being newly developed in the 17th century. Ever since Lock & Co. Hatters has moved with the times and today provides traditional, functional pieces as well as new fashions for both men and women, with everything from tweed hats and riding caps to cloches and fedoras.

PAXTON & WHITFIELD

Wedding cheese cake anyone?

93 Jermyn Street (SW1Y 6JE) / +44 (0)20 7930 0259
paxtonandwhitfield.co.uk / Open daily

Yet another purveyor with a history dating back to the mid-1700's. Don't you just love London? Although founded by the Cullum family, it is the family names of two later business partners that hang above the door. Never mind eating cake, Queen Victoria granted them a royal warrant (the first of a few) in 1850 and ate cheese instead. When the going got tough during the Second World War, with milk in short supply, Paxton & Whitfield became an "ordinary grocer". There's a lesson to be learnt in survival from this tiny outlet: change with the times and stay in business. Thankfully, they reverted to specializing in good cheese, and as Winston Churchill once remarked, "A gentleman buys ... his cheese at Paxton & Whitfield". With produce from rural cheesemakers across Britain, they also have a partnership with Androuet in Paris, to stock a range of French cheese while their finest Brit cheeses are sold in the French capital.

PETER EDWARDS

Extraordinary jewels

26 Conduit Street (W1S 2XX) / +44 (0)20 7491 1589
peteredwardsjewels.com / Closed Saturday and Sunday

Peter Edwards is a rarity himself. A true gentleman who has faithfully stuck to what is beautiful and rare in the way of Art Deco and 20th-century jewelry. In fact, I can think of no man who knows more about the subject. The grace and elegance of his vintage high-end shop is perfectly complemented by Noriko Yoshikawa, his partner, and their passion for great pieces of jewelry is infectious. Browsing the antique necklaces, rings, pins and earrings here is a lesson in 20th-century design fashions, and also stocked are pieces by leading individual designers such as Rene Boivin, Paul Flato and Pierre Sterle.

PHILIP MOULD

Dealer of notable British art and Old Master portraits

29 Dover Street (W1S 4NA) / +44 (0)20 7499 6818 / philipmould.com
Closed Saturday and Sunday

Philip Mould is a treasure-hunter of note; a modern-day sleuth of fine art. Along with Bendor Grosvenor, who heads up the gallery's research department (and writes an entertaining art blog) this is the most formidable team in rediscovering lost van Dycks, Gainsboroughs and such like – so-called "sleepers" that have lain unrecognized for decades. Even if your wallet doesn't stretch quite as far as taking home a masterpiece, aspirational collectors or anyone with artistic interests should make a visit to the gallery: it's a mini-museum of British art and there are regular exhibitions of works from the 16th century through to today.

SCOTTS

First-class seafood and fresh fish

20 Mount Street (W1K 2HE) / +44 (0)20 7495 7309
scotts-restaurant.com / Open daily

I have been known, on several occasions, to have had lunch here and simply stayed for dinner. The kitchen consistently serves stellar fish and seafood, the Champagne flows freely and it's a people-watcher's delight. This vibey, upmarket British eatery put Mount Street back on the map. There is nothing staid or obnoxious about it. I struggle not to order the slip soles (baby soles, which are incredibly delicate) on every single visit, and when the Jerusalem artichokes are in season, they're a must. My daughter Sofia claims they serve the very best mash potato in town. To round it off (or indeed oneself), the Bakewell Tart is quite simply marvelous. Few restaurants pay as much attention to their desserts.

SMYTHSON

Leather and paper heaven

40 New Bond Street (W1S 2DE) / +44 (0)20 7629 8558
smythson.com / Open daily

The 125 years for which they have been selling luxury leather-bound diaries and journals make this an institution. No traveler should be without a "featherweight" Smythson (and ideally one with your initials embossed, in gold), offered in a range of gloriously decadent colors (or black if you like a classic). Fittingly, the pretty, dusty blue presentation boxes with their branded ribbon make these ideal gifts for anyone. They also have personalized stationery if you really want to push the boat out and stunning jewelry boxes and travel cases. I love their fun-titled waffer notebooks, amongst which you can find anything from "Love Letters" to "Make it Happen" to "Over the Moon".

afternoon tea spots

The very agreeable English ceremony

BROWN'S HOTEL
33 Albemarle Street (W1S 4BP), +44 (0)20 7493 6020
roccofortehotels.com, daily, tea noon – 6pm

LOUIS HUNGARIAN PATISSERIE
32 Heath Street (NW3 6TE), +44 (0)20 7435 9908
facebook.com/LouisBakeryTeaRoom, open daily

ORANGE PEKOE
3 White Hart Lane (SW13 0PX), +44 (0)20 8876 6070
orangepekoeteas.com, daily, tea 2pm – 5pm

SKETCH
9 Conduit Street (W1S 2XG), +44 (0)20 7659 4500, sketch.uk.com
daily, tea 12.30pm – 6pm

ST JAMES HOTEL AND CLUB
7-8 Park Place (SW1A 1LS), +44 (0)20 7629 7688
stjameshotelandclub.com, daily, tea 3pm – 5.30pm

THE MODERN PANTRY
47-48 St John's Square (EC1V 4JJ), +44 (0)20 7553 9210
themodernpantry.co.uk, open daily

THE ORANGERY
Kensington Palace, Kensington Gardens (W8 4PX)
+44 (0)20 3166 6113, orangerykensingtonpalace.co.uk
daily, tea 2pm – 5pm

THE TEA ROOMS
155 Stoke Newington (N16 0UH), +44 (0)20 7923 1870
thetearooms.org, open daily

Everyone knows that Brits are partial to a bit of afternoon tea drinking, myself included. For a classic rendition, **St James Hotel and Club** offers various infusions with scones, jams and pastries by Chef William Drabble. As the oldest hotel in London, **Brown's Hotel** is steeped in history (including Queen Victoria taking tea here) and in the English Tea Room they serve a choice of 17 brews in antique silver. Another good bet is **The Orangery** at Kensington Palace, which affords an 18th-century view of the palace's gardens while you enjoy your refreshments.

If tempted by a village atmosphere, head over to Barnes in the west and **Orange Pekoe**. On lovely vintage china, tuck into finger sandwiches, scones with jam and Cornish clotted cream and a selection of decadent cakes. Or top off an afternoon walk

SKETCH

on Hampstead Heath at **Louis Hungarian Patisserie** – the pastries are shown to you on a tray, for making that tricky choice, alongside your silver teapot.

Visit Stoke Newington to find **The Tea Rooms**, where everything is homemade so give them a ring the day before you would like to enjoy your freshly baked full afternoon tea.

Fancy something a little more innovative? Then **The Modern Pantry**'s take on tea could be perfect – the Darjeeling and pink peppercorn scones come with clotted cream and berry and licorice jam. For wow factor, though, **Sketch** is hard to beat – on weekdays in the Glade, or on weekends in the Martin Creed Gallery Restaurant, afternoon indulgence here is spectacular.

BROWN'S HOTEL

knightsbridge and belgravia

pimlico

When Oscar Wilde was arrested for "gross indecency with other men" it was in a Knightsbridge hotel. When Mike Bloomberg decided to blow $10 million on a London townhouse, it was just around the corner from there. When millions of tourists want to shop till they drop, they do so along Brompton Road and its boutique-lined tributaries. From famous crimes and more famous department stores (Harrods) and the UK's most expensive rental property (One Hyde Park) to practically every ambassador's residence in the country, Knightsbridge and Belgravia are about as swish as it gets. Delve beyond the ultra luxe exterior and you'll find some of this city's coziest pubs, quiet gardens and all sorts of indie (if upmarket) retailers and enterprises worth at the very least a short exercise in wistful window shopping.

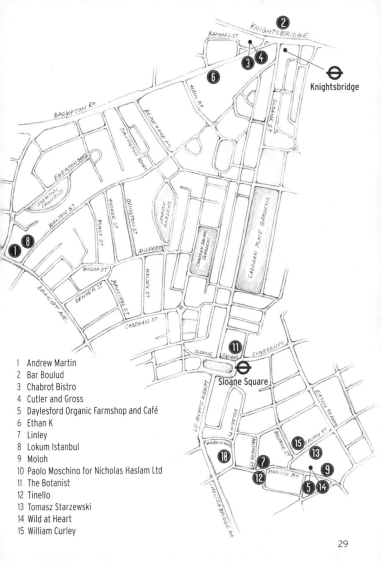

1 Andrew Martin
2 Bar Boulud
3 Chabrot Bistro
4 Cutler and Gross
5 Daylesford Organic Farmshop and Café
6 Ethan K
7 Linley
8 Lokum Istanbul
9 Moloh
10 Paolo Moschino for Nicholas Haslam Ltd
11 The Botanist
12 Tinello
13 Tomasz Starzewski
14 Wild at Heart
15 William Curley

198–200 Walton Street (SW3 2JL) / +44 (0)20 7225 5100
andrewmartin.co.uk / Closed Sunday

This rambling space with its quirky array of furniture and decorative pieces is one of my favorite interior design shops. Where else can one find the nose and cockpit of a fighter plane or a vintage pinball machine? There is also lighting, bedding, furniture, accessories and fabrics inspired by many different cultures and decades, but it's their fun and funky wallpaper collection that really stands out for me. Co-founded by Martin Waller in 1978, this homegrown establishment is today an international brand but remains true to its principles of blending styles from cultures around the globe, for eclectic yet elegant living.

BAR BOULUD

Upscale burgers

Mandarin Oriental Hyde Park, 66 Knightsbridge (SW1X 7LA)
+44 (0)20 7201 3899 / barboulud.com/London / Open daily

Daniel Boulud's London eatery is a gastro bolt-hole in the middle of the hum-drum, well hidden down a side entrance to the Mandarin Oriental hotel. First introduced to this French-American bistro by my friend Alice, I was already a fan of Boulud's restaurants in New York and here this Frenchman brings some very classy burgers to London – they are an absolute joy. So much so that I have often ordered three different ones to share between two. They are, thankfully, decidedly French in size but incredibly juicy, and appear with such indulgent toppings as confit pork belly, BBQ pulled pork and green chili, or foie gras with red wine braised short ribs. There is no better late night snack in town, and the bar is open until 1am.

CHABROT BISTROT

Quintessentially French eatery

9 Knightsbridge Green (SW1X 7QL) / +44 (0)20 7225 2238
chabrot.com / Open daily

It's almost too easy to miss this little bistro in a small alleyway along the side of the very glamorous Bulgari Hotel. I'd never have ventured in had it not been for a restaurateur acquaintance, who took me there for what turned out to be a wonderful meal. In the heart of London's most expensive neighborhood, this place is refreshingly reasonable on the wallet, as well as evoking the holiday flavors of Southwest France. This is classic French food, including the staples done well and my top picks: the homemade foie gras, stuffed cabbage with veal and, of course, a dozen oysters. The wine list is as you'd expect, very French, to perfectly complement your authentic culinary experience.

CUTLER AND GROSS

The world through rose-colored specs

16 Knightsbridge Green (SW1X 7QL) / +44 (0)20 7581 2250
cutlerandgross.com / Open daily

It's all my friend Bob's fault; I should never have asked which brand of glasses he always wears. Since then, many a pair of shades from Cutler and Gross have become faithful travel companions of mine. My buffalo-horn-framed ones are still my most prized, but there are quite a few more. This handcrafted frame company started life in 1969 in the heart of Knightsbridge and that's where you'll still find them today. Tony Gross and Graham Cutler are the founders of what is the brilliant yet discreet British eyewear brand. Today you can visit not just their shop but their museum, which displays hundreds of original designs. They support campaigns including the Elton John AIDS Foundation and as I'm sure you've already guessed, yes, his glasses are from here too.

DAYLESFORD ORGANIC FARMSHOP AND CAFÉ

From farm to shop and plate

44B Pimlico Road (SW1W 8LP) / +44 (0)20 7881 8060
daylesford.com / Open daily

For over 30 years the Bamford family has farmed organically, and this shop and café brings their produce to the city, along with Carole Bamford's passion for healthy living. What they don't produce themselves (which is a lot – meat, poultry, veggies, bakery and dairy), they source from other like-minded artisan suppliers. This is no grungy shed-like farm outlet with a few apples in a basket, though, but an organic boutique. The marble shelving throughout is beautiful and for a bite to eat you have the option of outside (weather permitting) or inside, downstairs or upstairs. I can't leave this establishment without a basket of organic cheese and some suitable crackers or flatbread along with a homemade chutney.

ETHAN K

Exotic skins expertise

Harrods, 87-135 Brompton Road (SW1X 7XL) / +44 (0)20 7730 1234
ethan-k.com / Open daily

This young Singaporean-born entrepreneur is taking the city by storm with his handcrafted, crocodile- and snake-skin travel bags and clutches. A fourth generation tanner, Ethan Koh came to London to study at the prestigious Central Saint Martins College of Arts and Design and decided to create a few one-off bags in his free time. Now, his masterpieces can be found in the windows of Harrods and on the arms of many well-known fashionistas. I'm suggesting you check out the concession in Harrods, although for the true Ethan K experience you should really arrange to visit his studio, just off Sloane Square, and treat yourself to a one-of-a-kind made-to-measure handbag.

LINLEY

Showcase of English carpentry and cabinetry

60 Pimlico Road (SW1W 8LP) / +44 (0)20 7730 7300 / davidlinley.com
Closed Sunday

From the outside Linley is a row of immaculate white terraced houses, with stunning window displays, especially during London events such as the Wimbledon Championships and the Chelsea Flower Show. Stepping inside, you enter a cavernous aesthetic showroom. This pinnacle of British furniture and interiors, established by David Linley in 1985, is recognized for the highest quality craftsmanship. It offers everything from sterling silver mustard jar tops and gorgeous wooden photo frames to study desks, dining rooms and even super-yacht fit-outs. The store gives you a sense of David's own passion and wit in its curated collection of superb design and artistry.

LOKUM ISTANBUL

Turkish delight in the literal sense

95 Walton Street (SW3 2HP) / +44 (0)20 7225 0705
lokumistanbul.co.uk / Open daily

This company is the personal drive by Zeynep Keyman to resurrect the culinary luxuries of the Ottoman-Turkish culture. The entire boutique is a passage in time, filled with the most exquisite boxes of Turkish delight, the beauty of which rival the decadent design of the store itself. But it's not only delicate confectionery; they also stock cologne water and candles that are equally wonderful. The finesse and detailing of what is offered here is a joy to behold, and such a pleasure to see in our increasingly standardized, banal world.

MOLOH

English-wear from the countryside to the city

24 Pimlico Road (SW1W 8LJ) / +44 (0)20 7730 0430 / moloh.com
Closed Sunday

Exclusively designed and made in the UK, Moloh (the name of owner Caroline's chocolate Labrador) represents small-business, skillfully made fashion. This is quintessential Britishness, traditionally influenced, with a twist — jackets, coats and waistcoats are tailored with just enough eccentricity to make them interesting yet sophisticated. Sadly they don't offer menswear but that hasn't stopped me from buying several embroidered belts and belt buckles (sold separately). Based, as one would expect, in the countryside, we are ever so grateful they also have a shop in town.

PAOLO MOSCHINO FOR NICHOLAS HASLAM LTD

Understated interiors glamour

12-14 Holbein Place (SW1W 8NL)   +44 (0)20 7730 8623
nicholashaslam.com / Closed Sunday

Paolo Moschino worked with Nicky Haslam, one of the UK's top interior designers, for six years before taking over this retail business (established in 1980). Creating modern yet traditional interiors, with inspiration from his Italian home, Paolo is a self-confessed shopaholic as well as talented designer. The showroom is elegantly packed with plush furnishings and classy accessories. It's here I most often pick up a great piece of ceramic or a lamp or even a pair of Belgian shoes. The items they offer are classicly stylish and chic without being old fashioned. You can also find them at the Design Centre Chelsea Harbour but the two main outlets are around the corner from each other in Pimlico.

THE BOTANIST

Very Chelsea

7 Sloane Square (SW1W 8EE) / +44 (0)20 7730 0077
thebotanistonsloanesquare.com / Open daily

Covered in old botanical drawings, this bar and restaurant is a rather smart affair. It gets pretty busy, which I always class as a good sign, but the service is some of the slickest I have ever experienced and the food is first-rate simple British cooking. The seabass and mango ceviche with smoked chili salt is a dish I recommend, or opt for their grilled lobster with garlic and tarragon butter and hand-cut chips. The fish and seafood is, by the way, hand-picked every morning at Billingsgate Fish Market. You could go to The Botanist for any occasion: breakfast, brunch, lunch, dinner, or just to unwind with one of their specialized cocktails – and Sloane Square is a top spot to indulge in a little people-watching while you do so.

TINELLO

Pared-down modern Italian

87 Pimlico Road (SW1W 8PH) / +44 (0)20 7730 3663 / tinello.co.uk
Closed Sunday

Often, on one of my days of browsing the interior décor shops in the near-by area, I will end up at Tinello for lunch. My suggestion, in this no fuss but chic Italian eatery, is to order a number of the small plates and share. I can't go without the Tuscan chicken liver crostini, the burrata with pomegranate and, whenever it's on offer, the lardo crostini with thyme honey. The menu, naturally, changes according to season, but I always love their pasta dishes and I know I can recommend the beef, however it might be presented when you're there.

TOMASZ STARZEWSKI

Chic elegance in the making

229 Ebury Street (SW1W 8UT) / +44 (0)20 7730 8886
starzewski.com / Open Monday to Friday, or by appointment

Polish-British designer Tomasz Starzewski owns this couture boutique that offers women the most glamorous and elegant gowns and tailoring. It's a discreet place with royalty amongst its patronage, and Tomasz's stunning creations have made an entrance on the likes of the late Princess Diana. Couture and ready-to-wear clothing is made on the premises – now who still does that in this day and age in central London? – and you can browse the pieces displayed with flair. Not only that, but there is also an interiors side of the business, which showcases lovely materials and a number of other artists including Emma Sergeant.

WILD AT HEART

Locally grown and seasonal

30A Pimlico Road (SW1W 8LJ) / +44 (0)20 7229 1174
wildatheart.com / Closed Sunday

Where in the capital do flower arrangements get any better than here?
I love the name but I love even more what they do with the most beautiful
blooms. Nikki Tibbles started her company 20 years ago and now has two
shops and a concession at Liberty (pg 98). Wild at Heart concentrates on
locally grown, seasonal flowers, offering bouquets and displays that are
fresh and vibrant. Nikki also has an ever-increasing line of homewares and
I often leave her shop with a vase or two for the flowers I've bought.

WILLIAM CURLEY

Chocolate heaven on Earth

198 Ebury Street (SW1W 8UN) / +44 (0)20 8538 9650
williamcurley.com / Open daily

Since 2007 this Scottish husband and Japanese wife team have won the award for Britain's Best Chocolatiers numerous times. They both had distinguished careers at equally distinguished establishments that led them towards this, the most fabulous chocolate boutique and dessert bar. In terms of straightforward chocolate, their dark 65% and 70% is heavenly, or for those with a sweeter tooth, try the sea salt caramel dark chocolate or the dark chocolate honeycomb. For the more adventurous there is an array of Asian-influenced combinations using green tea or sake, just for example. And then there's the pâtisserie – the dessert bar is open Saturday and Sunday afternoons, for some cocoa indulgence more divine than anywhere else on Earth.

quintessential pubs

When in London...

THE GRAZING GOAT
6 New Quebec Street (W1H 7RQ), +44 (0)20 7724 7243
thegrazinggoat.co.uk, open daily

THE HOLLY BUSH
22 Holly Mount (NW3 6SG), +44 (0)20 7435 2892
hollybushhampstead.co.uk, open daily

THE LAMB AND FLAG
33 Rose Street (WC2E 9EB), +44 (0)20 7497 9504
lambandflagcoventgarden.co.uk, open daily

THE MAYFLOWER
117 Rotherhithe Street (SE16 4NF), +44 (0)20 7237 4088
themayflowerrotherhithe.com, open daily

THE THOMAS CUBITT
44 Elizabeth Street (SW1W 9PA), +44 (0)20 7730 6060
thethomascubitt.co.uk, open daily

THE WHITE HORSE
1–3 Parsons Green (SW6 4UL), +44 (0)20 7736 2115
whitehorsesw6.com, open daily

YE OLDE CHESHIRE CHEESE
145 Fleet Street (EC4A 2BU), +44 (0)20 7353 6170
no website, closed Sunday

THE LAMB AND FLAG

London folk do enjoy a trip to a public house, and with over 7,000 watering holes to choose from, it might be rude not to join them.

For a historic drinking establishment, it's difficult to beat **Ye Olde Cheshire Cheese** (pg 112), but **The Lamb and Flag** in Covent Garden is another not to miss – previous regulars include Charles Dickens, and the alleyway beside it witnessed poet John Dryden being mugged in 1679. But fear not, it's now perfectly charming.

A little further afield, up in Hampstead, **The Holly Bush** has long been one of the greatest pubs in London. North from the main village High Street, this place serves good food as well as real ale. Or across town in Rotherhithe is another public house of old: **The Mayflower** (established 1621) is the oldest pub on the River Thames, and you can take in the view from their jetty with blankets and hot water bottle supplied in case it's chilly.

THE HOLLY BUSH

VIEW FROM THE MAYFLOWER

Over in west London, **The White Horse**, affectionately known as "The Sloaney Pony", welcomes pint drinkers, good food eaters, young professionals and families and accompanying dogs in their beer garden, or in their big leather sofas inside, or at the dining tables in the former coach house. While a similar ex-inn public house and hotel, **The Grazing Goat**, is ideally placed for stopping off at after battling the shops on Oxford Street, or even before your assault as they offer breakfast from 7.30am.

Last but in no way least is **The Thomas Cubitt**, a fine Belgravia gastropub. From the wood-paneled bar to the elegant white table-clothed dining room, this is no gloomy old pub, but a place you can eat your traditional roast or posh fish and chips in bright sunlit comfort.

chelsea

For fans of luxury sports cars, a walk along Chelsea's main drag, King's Road, can be a gawk fest. Of course most of the Ferraris, Lamborghinis, Maseratis et al that you'll see will be moving along at a snail's pace and hardly able to get out of first gear due to all the traffic. An opportunity to revel in schadenfreude or perhaps to take a closer look at some of the world's most sophisticated metallic beasts? You decide. One thing's for sure though, wealth courses through this upmarket artery of West London life. If all the revving on King's Road gets to be too much, a quick detour down pretty much any side street will soon reveal a quieter, if still rather posh, side of Chelsea. Here the Royal Hospital for retired veterans plays host to a famous flower show attracting global attention and the Thames rolls along with ease, with leafy Battersea Park and its Peace Pagoda across the river on its southern shore.

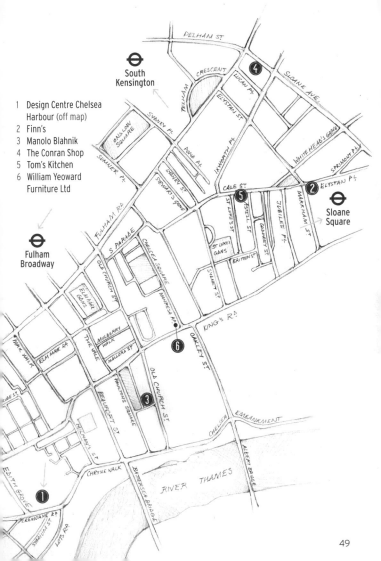

1 Design Centre Chelsea
   Harbour (off map)
2 Finn's
3 Manolo Blahnik
4 The Conran Shop
5 Tom's Kitchen
6 William Yeoward
   Furniture Ltd

DESIGN CENTRE CHELSEA HARBOUR

The land of design

411-412 Design Centre East (SW10 0XF) / +44 (0)20 7225 9166
dcch.co.uk / Closed Saturday and Sunday

There is little that is old-world about the Design Centre at Chelsea Harbour, other than how it is built on the banks of and overlooks the River Thames. Three enormous domed galleries house dozens of British and international interior décor shops, with an enormous range of wallpapers, fabrics, light fittings and other furnishings. It's a designer's dream come true. There are also two little gems within the center: namely The Bookshop, which stocks all the latest design and interiors books, and a wonderful restaurant, Design Café, which generally serves organic food. A first-rate hangout on a rainy day.

FINN'S

Fresh, tasty food on the green

4 Elystan Street (SW3 3NS) / +44 (0)20 7225 0733
finnsofchelseagreen.com / Closed Sunday

A "one family, two generations" run deli and café, Finn's is tucked away on Chelsea Green, a few yards back from the buzz on King's Road. This little delight is heading towards its 30th anniversary and is still feeding the local community. I often grab one of the four tiny tables for a freshly cooked lunch (including an irresistible dessert) if shopping in the area and invariably walk out with several hundred grams of their cut-off-the-bone, home-cooked ham and a selection of their homemade pâtés. They also always have a few knickknacks such as hand-blown perfume bottles or handmade placemats, which find their way into my shopping bags.

MANOLO BLAHNIK

The home of gorgeous heels

49-51 Old Church Street (SW3 5BS) / +44 (0)20 7352 8622
manoloblahnik.com

At a conference, I remember journalist Suzy Menkes introducing
Manolo Blahnik as "the last great Emperor of shoes". When this craftsman
extraordinaire spoke, I was so inspired by his humble yet passionate devotion
to his art that I decided to visit his showroom in Chelsea, his flagship store
that he has operated from since 1973. It's amazing to think that from this
little place Manolo revolutionized women's footwear with his elegant heels.
Indeed, entirely convinced he only designed shoes for women, I took along
someone I was going to buy a pair for, on my first visit. To my utter delight I
found he does do a few designs for men, so we both departed this tiny store
as happy shoppers and Blahnik converts!

THE CONRAN SHOP

Supreme design store in an iconic building

81 Fulham Road, Michelin House (SW3 6RD) / +44 (0)20 7589 7401
conranshop.co.uk / Open daily

On Saturdays I avoid the shops; there are far too many other shoppers. But on Sunday, from noon onwards, I can often be found at The Conran Shop. It's one of those enormous emporiums of design, full of seriously cool stuff. Founded by Terence Conran in 1974, the Chelsea shop proudly stands in the former Michelin building. As the founder of Habitat in the mid-1960's, Conran is a name synonymous with design in the UK and I love his philosophy: "good design gives you pleasure and improves the quality of all our lives through products, buildings or interiors that work well, are affordable and look beautiful." I've bought dozens of birthday and Christmas gifts here over the years: everything from ostrich feather dusters to wooden board games.

TOM'S KITCHEN

Flying the flag for Brit comfort food

**27 Cale Street (SW3 3QP) / +44 (0)20 7349 0202 / tomskitchen.co.uk
Open daily**

Chef Tom Aiken comes from a line of wine merchants but cooking is
what grabbed his interest as a teenager, and he now has several restaurants
in London. Tom's Kitchen is a bastion of organic British-produced comfort
grub, such as classic fish pie or their seven-hour-confit lamb for sharing.
There's passion in the sourcing of ingredients, the cooking and the environment
it's produced and consumed in. This is a relaxed, family-friendly oasis.
A supporter of numerous charities, Tom refuses to sell tuna or swordfish in
his restaurants, and instead supports the use of less threatened, local fish.
His own fishing boat is suitably named Maximus Sustainable.

WILLIAM YEOWARD FURNITURE LTD

The style-maker of King's Road

270 King's Road (SW3 5AW) / +44 (0)20 7349 7828
williamyeoward.com / Open daily

In an ideal world, William Yeoward should kit out your entire home. This designer of note has, since the 1980's, created and sold handsome accessories, furniture and glassware along with wallpaper and rugs. I'd take it all. The secret I believe of his success is that he designs things he'd want in his own home. William has also written several books ranging from interior décor to table settings and the American bar. But if you are worried about buying something because it might break on your return flight home, fear not, as you can order online too. One of my most outrageous purchases: three-dozen ceramic fish.

london after dark

Swanky cocktail hangouts

BINCHO-MIZUWARI
16 Old Compton Street (W1D 4TL), +44 (0)20 7287 9111
bincho.co.uk, closed Sunday

RONNIE SCOTT'S JAZZ CLUB
47 Frith Street (W1D 4HT), +44 (0)20 7439 0747
ronniescotts.co.uk, open daily

RUBY'S
76 Stoke Newington Street (N16 7XB), rubysdalston.com
closed Sunday and Monday

THE HIDE
39–45 Bermondsey Street (SE1 3XF), +44 (0)20 7403 6655
thehidebar.com, closed Sunday and Monday

WORSHIP STREET WHISTLING SHOP
63 Worship Street (EC2A 2DU), +44 (0)20 7247 0015
whistlingshop.com, closed Sunday and Monday

Thankfully, this city has a fantastic supply of bars to keep the swarms of thirsty locals as well as the visitors happy, and well into the small hours, too.

One of the most inventive bars in town is **Worship Street Whistling Shop** in Shoreditch – combining Victorian atmosphere and 21st-century style, here the drinks menu is somewhat scientific, coming with its own glossary. Luckily the mixologists are highly knowledgeable about their concoctions, and can explain all ingredients for these carefully crafted tipples. Not to be outdone though, Dalston's **Ruby's** is also charmingly quirky. They serve Mojitos in 1940's milk bottles and I say they make the classiest Manhattans in London.

Another favorite of mine is South London's **The Hide**. Award-winning bartenders and some of the city's most tempting cocktails, plus tasty snacks served til 11pm can make for a fabulous evening.

If you're feeling a little on the wild side, head to the whisky bar at **Bincho-Mizuwari**, in the basement below an Izakaya restaurant. At this trendy Soho spot you can find rare Japanese whiskies that will give you a few extra hairs on your chest. While in the West End, make sure to include the late show at **Ronnie Scott's Jazz Club** in your night, where countless big names have played and Jimi Hendrix gave his last live gig. Seated at one of their tables with a red lamp, you'll be well-placed to enjoy the best live jazz in town.

WORSHIP STREET WHISTLING SHOP

kensington

south kensington, holland park

———◆———

Searching for some semblance of London as seen in *Mary Poppins*? Kensington, with its ivied mews and row upon row of white Victorian mansions, is probably the ideal place to do it. It's also a brilliant spot for afternoon tea in the park and for a day of wide-eyed wonder visiting the area's Museum Quarter. Kensington is home to Hyde Park, Holland Park and Kensington Gardens, and the Victoria & Albert Museum, with a collection of art and design stretching from 3,000 years ago to the most current of contemporary trends, the family friendly Science Museum, and the grandiose Natural History Museum – all free to visit. It's not all Disney-esque and kid-centric though. Shopping here can be a very grown-up affair along the retail row of the High Street and the boutiques. A bounty of excellent pubs and quality restaurants awaits as well.

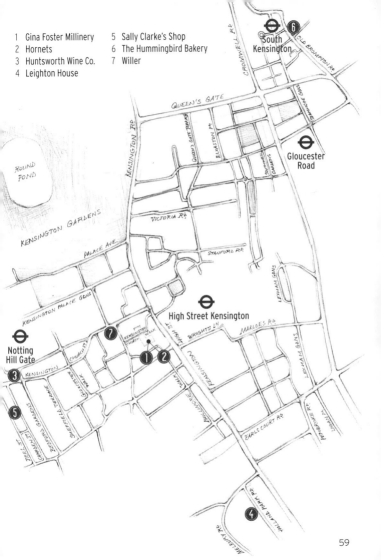

1 Gina Foster Millinery
2 Hornets
3 Huntsworth Wine Co.
4 Leighton House
5 Sally Clarke's Shop
6 The Hummingbird Bakery
7 Willer

GINA FOSTER MILLINERY

Delicate and glamorous hats for ladies

5 Kensington Church Walk (W8 4NB) / +44 (0)20 7937 7611
ginafoster.co.uk / Closed Sunday

Hidden from the passing throng on Kensington High Street, down a
narrow but ever so quaint pedestrian walk, is this tiny hat shop, from
where Gina Foster has supplied everyone from film stars and royalty,
to brides and fashionistas with fabulous headwear. Her hats can be
customized and bespoke made, and her range extends to headdresses
and fascinators, and a gorgeous range of clutches too. When friends
are faced with attending a society do that requires headdress, I always
direct them here.

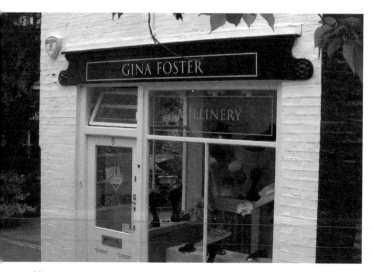

HORNETS

Vintage clothing for the dandy

2 & 4 Kensington Church Walk (W8 4NB) / +44 (0)20 7937 1515
hornetskensington.co.uk / Open daily

Another gem tucked away in Kensington, this is the place where men can
become gentlemen. The charmingly eccentric Englishmen that run the
three mini-boutiques that make up Hornets offer an eclectic mix of vintage
clothes and accessories. Crammed into these shops is everything from ties
and cufflinks, to second-hand Panama hats and brogues, along with a good
dose of advice and conversation. I particular love the hats and almost always
walk out with a vintage Herbert Johnson and a Christys'. If you're new to
town but fancy looking like you're a born, bred and well-heeled British gent,
here is your chance to get kitted out, and for a humble price, too.

HUNTSWORTH WINE CO.

Boutique vino shop

**108 Kensington Church Street (W8 4BH) / +44 (0)20 7229 1602
huntsworthwine.co.uk / Closed Sunday**

As a firm supporter of independent establishments, this supplier of wine on Kensington Church Street (which had a previous guise, under the same owner and his mother, as an antiques business) is one of my top recommendations. Although they specialize in wines from Bordeaux, owner Tuggy Meyer ensures an interesting selection from across the globe is available. Huntsworth Wine Co. offers not only the finest French reds but also a wide selection of lesser-known but equally enjoyable bottles. And, not to be partisan about it, anything they don't happen to have on the shelves, they're always happy to source. One extra tip: after finding your perfect bottle you can then pop to the shop across the road and find some lovely vintage glassware to drink it from.

LEIGHTON HOUSE

An untouched Victorian artist's home

12 Holland Park (W14 8LZ) / +44 (0)20 7602 3316
rbkc.gov.uk/subsites/museums/leightonhousemuseum1.aspx
Closed Tuesdays

Frederic, Lord Leighton's former home and studio isn't far from busy Kensington High Street but provides an oasis of tranquility and architectural interest. As a painter, Leighton is not only one of the most famous British artists of the Victorian Era, he is also one of my firm favorites. The house has the outward appearance of an Italian palazzo, but step within and you'll discover the spectacular, tiled and gilded Arab Hall, modeled on a 12th-century palace in Sicily. With its two-story golden dome, intricate mosaics, Islamic tiles and central fountain, it's probably not what you were expecting to find in genteel Kensington. There are some of Leighton's works on show, and some he owned by other artists, as well as regular exhibitions.

SALLY CLARKE'S SHOP

London's baker of note

1 Campden Street (W8 7EP) / +44 (0)20 7229 2190
sallyclarke.com / Open daily

Since the mid-'80s, Sally Clarke has been creating and serving terrific meals at her well-known "no choice" restaurant on Kensington Church Street. However, I'm most indebted to her for opening a shop and bakery from where she serves not only the local community but also some of the foremost hotels in London and the Houses of Parliament, no less. Indulge yourself in choosing from the splendid array of pastries, tarts and cakes – the lemon meringue always smiles at me whenever I call in, although the carrot cake tells me it's somewhat healthier. And to take home with your heavenly smelling fresh bread, don't forget a couple of artisanal British cheeses, which must be enjoyed with some of that homemade chutney...

THE HUMMINGBIRD BAKERY

Cupcake lovers delight

47 Old Brompton Road (SW7 3JP) / +44 (0)20 7851 1795
hummingbirdbakery.com / Open daily

With pastry shops to be found across London, this sugary-sweet cupcake paradise offers freshly baked American-style goodies for delivery or pick up in-store, or for relishing alongside a cup of coffee. These wicked people have even gone as far as to offer a mobile unit: a bakery-on-wheels, to bring their entire range of desserts such as cheesecakes and whoopie pies to your front door – how enticingly easy! I always go for the perfectly classic red velvet or vanilla cupcakes, but if you'd like to try more flavors a selection of their mini treats might help you find your own top choice. And the "made without" range even offers some healthy options. Whether it's a little celebration or a bit of consolation, or simply because it's Tuesday, a cupcake pitstop in South Kensington is always welcome.

WILLER

Unique pieces for your home

**12 Holland Street (W8 4LT) / +44 (0)20 7937 3518 / willer.co.uk
Closed Sunday**

Sadly, it is seldom that you find truly special objects in today's big cities, but this gallery of glassware, ceramics, linens, furniture and other homewares manages to source some profoundly unusual, beautiful and usable pieces. Willer offers an eclectic selection ranging from antique objects to contemporary design, ceramic to steel. Expect to see Song Dynasty porcelain alongside contemporary Italian glassware, shelved above modernist wooden furniture. The Claudy Jongstra tapestries and weaves, in particular, are breathtaking and something I ponder over every time I have a browse. An exhibition space, as well as the sales gallery, is a place of inspiration for designers and browsers alike.

curry houses

From super hot to ultra haute, the best of South Asian cuisine

CAFÉ SPICE NAMASTÉ
16 Prescot Street (E1 8AZ), +44 (0)20 7488 9242, cafespice.co.uk
closed Sunday

DISHOOM
12 Upper St Martin's Lane (WC2H 9FB), +44 (0)20 7420 9320
dishoom.com, open daily

LAHORE KEBAB HOUSE
2-10 Umberston Street (E1 1PY), +44 (0)20 7481 9737
lahore-kebabhouse.com, open daily

NEEDOO GRILL
87 New Road (E1 1HH), +44 (0)20 7247 0648, needoogrill.co.uk
open daily

NEW TAYYABS
83-89 Fieldgate Street (E1 1JU), +44 (0)20 7247 8521
tayyabs.co.uk, open daily

TAMARIND OF MAYFAIR
20 Queen Street (W1J 5PR), +44 (0)20 7629 3561
tamarindrestaurant.com, open daily

THE CINNAMON CLUB
The Old Westminster Library
30-32 Great Smith Street (SW1P 3BU)
+44 (0)20 7222 2555, cinnamonclub.com, closed Sunday

Until fairly recently, the answer to where to find the top Indian restaurants in the world was not India but Britain. Some folks still reckon that's the case and, with the old guard still dishing out the standards with spicy aplomb and young talents offering a 21st-century take on what makes South Asian cuisine so yummy, theirs is a strong argument.

For an inexpensive and authentically cosmopolitan experience, head to Whitechapel, where the kings of the old-school curry reign. There's the cavernous **Needoo Grill** with 99p Seek kebabs (not to mention a fantastic vegetarian bhindi bhagi); **Lahore Kebab House** and its equally scrumptious and budget-friendly Punjabi-style dishes; and **New Tayyabs**, where the line around the corner offers insight into the most British of institutions: queuing (and try the lamb chops to find out if it was worth the wait).

Staying in Whitechapel but upscaling the setting, Chef Patron Cyrus Todiwala's award-winning ode to fiery flavor, **Café Spice Namasté**, beckons those in search of a delicious blend of innovation and tradition.

Moving westward, **The Cinnamon Club** brings fine dining finesse with an avant garde approach to its white linen swathed tables. Set within the Old Westminster Library, it's an attractive venue and prime politician-spotting terrain. For another Michelin-starred curry "joint", head to **Tamarind of Mayfair** (the first Indian restaurant ever to receive a Michelin star and still one of only six in the world) for traditional Moghul cuisine and impeccable service.

For a hip and frisky feast go to **Dishoom** and admire its kitsch décor while enjoying its menu of Bombay café treats.

THE CINNAMON CLUB

notting hill

westbourne grove, ladbroke grove

Despite A-list celebs starring in blockbuster movies about the place (not to mention all the A-list celebs who actually live here) and an almost constant onslaught of tourists clogging up the Tube stations and getting lost on their way to Portobello Market, this frisky little corner of West London somehow manages to retain much of the same appeal that brought it such worldwide attention. With an ever youthful and increasingly cosmopolitan air, you're as apt to hear American, Italian, French, Aussie, Kiwi (or insert your chosen expat nationality here) accents, as you are one that's British. A delectable variety of local eateries, independent shops, galleries and street vendors all reflect the diverse and rather well-heeled mix of folks who've claimed Notting Hill as their stomping ground.

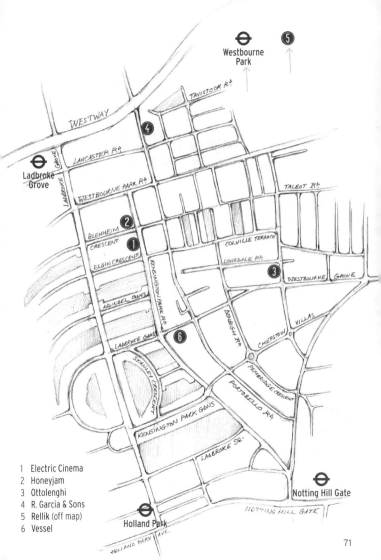

1 Electric Cinema
2 Honeyjam
3 Ottolenghi
4 R. Garcia & Sons
5 Rellik (off map)
6 Vessel

71

ELECTRIC CINEMA

The style in which films should be enjoyed

191 Portobello Road (W11 2ED) / +44 (0)20 7908 9696
electriccinema.co.uk / Open daily

An altogether different film-viewing experience is what you can expect to find at the Electric. Constructed in 1910, it was one of the first purpose-built cinemas in Britain, and having had a checkered career it's now back to its full former cinematic glory. Red sofas, foot-stalls and cashmere blankets offer luxurious, cozy, movie-watching comfort, with a theatrical, classical arch surrounding the screen and snazzy furnishings throughout. The Electric has a superb bar space, providing toothsome snacks and drinks to enjoy while you watch your chosen flick, which could be anything ranging from a block-buster to obscure art-house. One note of caution, I would advise booking your seats ahead of turning up, as this is one very popular cinema.

HONEYJAM

Old-fashioned toy store

2 Blenheim Crescent (W11 1NN) / +44 (0)20 7243 0449
honeyjam.co.uk / Open daily

Remember when you were little and you just had a few coins to buy a piece of candy at a toy store? Well, owners Jasmine Guinness and Honey Bowdrey remember, and they've recreated that experience at Honeyjam. While I was visiting, a little boy happily stocked up on some gobstoppers. Not only does this charming shop stock sweets, it also has a great selection of unusual toys and games, and on Tuesdays haircuts are offered by appointment. Though not a child's top choice of activity, it is so much more fun when a lollipop is offered at the end. As I wandered about, I mentally put together a goody bag for my goddaughter – fairy dust glitter, a kit to make a paper butterfly – all things that will help make her childhood a little more magical.

OTTOLENGHI

A treat for the eyes and the taste buds

**63 Ledbury Road (W11 2AD) / +44 (0)20 7727 1121 / ottolenghi.co.uk
Open daily**

Yotam Ottolenghi first opened what has become a godsend for many of us Londoners back in 2002. Now into its second decade, this dedicated and passionate team of culinary gurus continues to expand and grow with a few other restaurants in town, too. Their food is healthy, colorful and delicious. Yotam is Israeli and his dishes bring out notes of Middle Eastern and Mediterranean cookery – vegetables that evoke sunshine, cous cous, sesame, pomegranate, honey and plenty of olive oil. There are two things I especially love about this eatery: the vanilla rose cupcakes and the fact that they actively support several charities.

R. GARCIA & SONS

Family-owned Spanish grocery with history

**248-250 Portobello Road (W11 1LL) / +44 (0)20 7221 6119 /
rgarciaandsons.com / Open daily**

Whether you're in the area to sift through Ladbroke Grove's legendary
record stores, to do the Portobello antiques drag or merely to gawk
at Notting Hill's eclectic mix of tourists and locals, do yourself a favor
and drop by R. Garcia & Sons. While there, admire the hand-stacked
symmetry and vibrant labels along the aisles of this nearly 60-year-
old family-run grocery, and maybe pick up some of the best chorizo
and charcuterie to be found in the UK at the deli counter. For a quick
cortado, some authentic tapas, or a properly thick Spanish-style hot
chocolate, pay a visit to Garcia's next door café.

RELLIK

Ladies' vintage goldmine

8 Golborne Road (W10 5NW) / +44 (0)20 8962 0089
relliklondon.co.uk / Closed Sunday and Monday

For 14 years Fiona, Claire and Steven have run this ultimate dressing-up-box of a shop. On walking in you are greeted with rails of fabulous vintage clothing, ranging from lesser-known brands to the likes of Dior, Westwood, Gucci and YSL. Although you won't be short of vintage apparel outlets around London, Rellik offers something truly special. With one of the most discerning selections of clothing I have come across, they are kind enough to part with their dreamy pieces for very reasonable prices. So to accompany your stylish new look you can also choose from their glitzy, glamorous jewelry that is reliably eye-catching. I could go on and on about the treasures tucked away here, but I'll just warn you to give yourself plenty of browsing time.

VESSEL

A glass gem

114 Kensington Park Road (W11 2PW) / +44 (0)20 7727 8001
vesselgallery.com / Closed Sunday

This is truly an Aladdin's cave of glassware. Their own take on themselves is: "a gallery with the goods but without the attitude", which is indeed the perfect way to describe Vessel. Hidden just around the corner from Portobello Market, this two-floor store-cum-gallery is filled with unique pieces of crockery, stemware, cutlery, lighting and vases for every budget. You'll find everything from the funky to the flamboyant to the functional. There is always an exhibition on display and they take commissions for work on behalf of certain artists, too. If you're on the hunt for a present that is far from mundane, you'll find all sorts of good contenders here, or you can have a gift voucher sent direct to your lucky friend and give them the pleasure of choosing for themselves.

HAMPSTEAD HEATH
NW3, cityoflondon.gov.uk/things-to-do/green-spaces/
hampstead-heath, open daily

KENSINGTON ROOF GARDENS
99 Kensington High Street (W8 5SA), +44 (0)20 7937 7994
roofgardens.virgin.com, phone to check opening

POSTMAN'S PARK
St Martin's le Grand, Aldersgate Street and King Edward
Street (EC1), cityoflondon.gov.uk/things-to-do/green-spaces/
city-gardens, open daily

PRIMROSE HILL
NW1, +44 (0)300 061 2300
royalparks.org.uk/parks/the-regents-park, open daily

ST JAMES'S PARK
SW1A, +44 (0)300 061 2350
royalparks.org.uk/parks/st-jamess-park, open daily

ST JAMES'S PARK

parks and gardens

The green side of the city

Amid the constant buzz of the city, London offers plenty of chances to escape to lush and peaceful surroundings for a breather. As the neighbor of Buckingham Palace and the oldest of the capital's eight Royal Parks, **St James's Park** is a central spot for a stroll or a tranquil few minutes in a deck chair. Surrounded by historic buildings, there are outstanding views, a lake and a surprising variety of birdlife – not least the resident colony of pelicans.

If I am entertaining nature lovers in London, the **Kensington Roof Gardens** is the perfect place to wine and dine, whilst enjoying the serene settings of the Spanish, Tudor and English Woodland Gardens. There are over 70 full-size trees, a stream and flamingos, all 100 feet above Kensington High Street.

Every time I visit **Postman's Park**, not far from St Paul's Cathedral, I'm amazed by its peacefulness. It's truly a hidden gem in the busy working City area. Beautiful as much as it is historical, I never miss an opportunity to take a wander in this pocket of calm.

For one of the most panoramic views of London, stretch your legs up to the top of **Primrose Hill**, an off-shoot of the huge Regent's Park. And for combining a magnificent view of the city with what feels like a walk in the country, **Hampstead Heath** is the place. Including old woodland, grassy hills and ponds that feature swimmers from time to time, in any season, it's a fabulous place to be.

marylebone

You don't have be Sherlock Holmes, who fictitiously resided in the area (at 221B Baker Street, now a museum in his honor), to deduce that Marylebone achieves what so many London neighborhoods aim for but fall just short of: a village feel coupled with urban convenience. Much of its success rests on its enviable location. Wedged between the northeastern corner of Hyde Park and the southern end of Regent's Park with Tube stations aplenty scattered all around, Marylebone is as pedestrian friendly as central London gets. It's got the ever-bustling shopping mecca of Oxford Street separating it from Soho and Mayfair while exclusive Regent Street marks its border with Fitzrovia and cosmopolitan Edgware Road serves as its western extreme. Everything that's worthwhile and fun about those other areas seems to flow into this one, but in a low key, tempered and more manageable sort of manner.

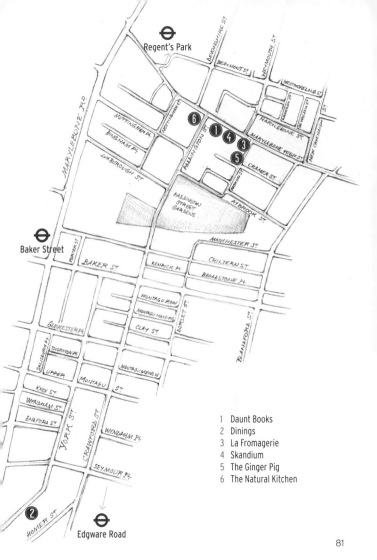

1 Daunt Books
2 Dinings
3 La Fromagerie
4 Skandium
5 The Ginger Pig
6 The Natural Kitchen

DAUNT BOOKS

Where the shelves are as lovely as the books on them

83-84 Marylebone High Street (W1U 4QW) / +44 (0)20 7224 2295
dauntbooks.co.uk / Open daily

Situated within its original Edwardian-era shop, Daunt Books is a historic and very pleasant destination in and of itself. Other than admiring the place, though, if you are actually here to shop, you're in luck – especially if you're keen to score some travel titles. Daunt has a good claim on being one of the premier travel-related bookstores in the world. Here, in the magnificently sky-lit back room, books are arranged geographically by relevant country. Can't find what you're looking for, or have any particular questions? The staff is extremely knowledgeable and more than willing to help, and not only for travel reads but also for other non-fiction and fiction, classic and new, all in this gloriously browse-worthy shop.

DININGS

Inventive Japanese cuisine

22 Harcourt Street (W1H 4HH) / +44 (0)20 7723 0666 / dinings.co.uk

In my opinion this contemporary restaurant is up there with the foremost for Japanese food in London. The décor may not be exciting, but there is nothing boring about the nosh here – it's fresh and innovative and, most importantly, tasty. There's strong Japanese authenticity behind the concept of Dinings' own tapas-type version of izakaya. The menu presents me with a problem, though: how to pick out any one of their dishes as a favorite, when they are all up there, as tantalizing as one another? I can say that the char-grilled Wagyu beef with Korean chili-miso is a real treat, and the selection of assorted sushi is as refreshing, light and delicious as sushi can be. With the service matching up to the high standard of the food, I can't recommend Dinings enough.

LA FROMAGERIE

Rustic cheese shop on an upscale high street

2-6 Moxon Street (W1U 4EW) / +44 (0)20 7935 0341
lafromagerie.co.uk / Open daily

Located in the very heart of Marylebone, La Fromagerie is as central as it gets. Still, somehow any visit feels like a trip to the countryside. With one of London's best butchers as a next-door neighbor and a farmers' market right outside its entrance every Sunday, it's a fine place to shop for foodie treats. And by "treats" I mean a gorgeous array of artisan cheeses from across Britain and Europe. But not only that! At La Fromagerie you'll also find seasonal and sustainably sourced fruits and vegetables alongside freshly baked breads, a delectable range of gourmet groceries and a smart selection of wine as well. With Regent's Park just a short stroll away, why not buy a picnic?

SKANDIUM

A Valhalla of delights for design-minded shoppers

86 Marylebone High Street (W1U 4QS) / +44 (0)20 7935 2077
skandium.com / Open daily

Fashionable Londoners have long looked to their Nordic neighbors for design and lifestyle inspiration. And those most en vogue know to go to Skandium for the most uplifting of Scandi insight. A British company, it was founded in 1999 by three Scandinavians to spread the gospel of how functionality and beauty can be achieved in harmony through a range of practical and attractive household items and furnishings. There is also a sister outlet nearby, devoted specifically to the furniture of designer Fritz Hansen, as well as another shop in Knightsbridge and a concession at Selfridges. But with its Dinesen flooring, massive skylight and internal courtyard, you'd be hard pressed to come across a more pleasing retail environment than this, the original shop, on Marylebone High Street.

THE GINGER PIG

Stalwarts of tradition and purveyors of quality cuts

8-10 Moxon Street (W1U 4EW) / +44 (0)20 7935 7788
thegingerpig.co.uk / Open daily

With two decades in the business of selling rare-breed meat reared
on more than 3,000 acres of the North York Moors, The Ginger Pig is
one of the best known and most highly respected bands of butchers
in all of Britain. You can pick up a choice cut for the grill but also grab
a quick and savory traditional English snack, such as a sausage roll.
Furthermore, if you really want to get to the meat of the matter, The
Ginger Pig offers a range of classes that allows the public behind the
counter and even the chopping block, as an entertaining, informative
and most welcome nothing-to-hide approach to promoting the
quality of their products.

THE NATURAL KITCHEN

Seasonal, organic, free-range shopping in a minimalist setting

77-78 Marylebone High Street (W1U 5JX) / +44 (0)20 3012 2123
thenaturalkitchen.com / Open daily

The Natural Kitchen is your one-stop shop and café for all things appetizing and healthy. With a communal-seated restaurant alongside a deli counter yielding a mouthwatering array of salads, cold cuts, soups, prepared foods, freshly made juices and more than commendably pulled espressos, the feel-good factor is high in this pared down and friendly grocery. The commitment to seasonal and sustainably sourced products and overall standards of every facet of any Natural Kitchen experience is always high, too. Prices are in line with expectations in this classy area and with the quality of the food, but the smiles and attentive service are free.

outdoor markets

Gaffs for all types of punters

BERWICK STREET MARKET
1 Berwick Street (W1F 0PH), no phone number
berwickstreetlondon.co.uk, closed Sunday

BOROUGH MARKET
8 Southwark Street (SE1 1TL), +44 (0)20 7407 1002
boroughmarket.org.uk, full market Wednesday to Saturday

BROADWAY MARKET
Broadway Market (E8 4PH), no phone number
broadwaymarket.co.uk, Saturday

COLUMBIA ROAD FLOWER MARKET
Columbia Road (E2 7RG), +44 (0)20 7613 0876
columbiaroad.info, Sunday

OLD SPITALFIELDS MARKET
16 Horner Square (E1 6EW), +44 (0)20 7247 8556
oldspitalfieldsmarkets.com, full market Thursday to Sunday

PIMLICO ROAD FARMERS MARKET
Orange Square (SW1W 8UT), no phone number
lfm.org.uk/markets/pimlico-road, Saturday

WHITECROSS STREET MARKET
Whitecross Street (EC1Y 8QJ), +44 (0)20 7378 0422
whitecrossstreet.co.uk, Thursday and Friday

Wandering around some of the city's oldest and largest markets will make you feel at home in London, and there's no better place to start than at **Columbia Road Flower Market**. In the east of the city, near Shoreditch, the market fills the street with stunning plants and flowers, with many independent shops alongside too. Also over east is **Broadway Market**, running between London Fields park and Regent's Canal, where the barrow boys of old now sell everything from organic meat and veg to bargain vintage clothing.

One of the capital's oldest markets is found bang in the middle of town, in Soho: **Berwick Street Market** offers an array of international food, British produce, clothing and leather goods. Another option for a heady fusion of global fare is the **Whitecross Street Market**, which appears near Barbican – make sure to find the funky burrito truck!

If you're after fresh, organic and direct-from-the-countryside food, **Pimlico Road Farmers Market** is well worth a visit. For rack upon rack of vintage clothes, antiques, vinyl and street art, **Old Spitalfields Market** is the place to go. Yet no discussion of markets would be complete without the incomparable **Borough Market** (pg 118) – unrivalled as a food-lover's paradise.

BOROUGH MARKET

west end

soho, covent garden

———◆———

As compellingly contemporary as it is utterly
historical, the ever-throbbing heart of London
does not disappoint. Home to what's arguably the
world's greatest assemblage of theaters and a highly
competitive line up of restaurants, clubs and watering
holes, the West End is the go-to area for a good time.
At its core is London's original Red Light District,
Soho, the epicenter of the LGBT scene – and thus the
city's hottest nightlife. But it's also a straight-friendly
destination at all times and a mostly fine place for kids
during daylight hours. The raucous streets of Soho
yield to a tiny yet teeming Chinatown and the never
tiring but often tiresome hub of Leicester Square.
Adjacent Covent Garden and the village-y retail enclave
of Seven Dials beckon a steady stream of locals and
tourists all keen to cavort in a setting where people
have been doing just that for centuries.

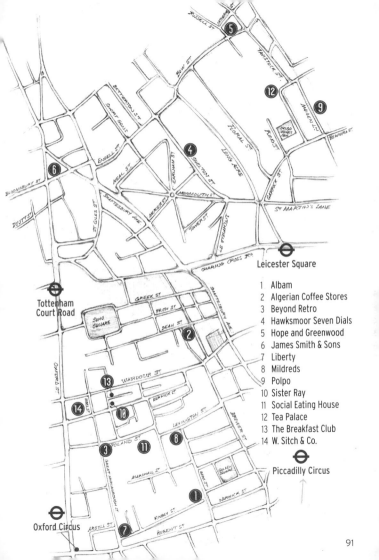

1 Albam
2 Algerian Coffee Stores
3 Beyond Retro
4 Hawksmoor Seven Dials
5 Hope and Greenwood
6 James Smith & Sons
7 Liberty
8 Mildreds
9 Polpo
10 Sister Ray
11 Social Eating House
12 Tea Palace
13 The Breakfast Club
14 W. Sitch & Co.

Leicester Square

Tottenham Court Road

Oxford Circus

Piccadilly Circus

ALBAM

More than comfy clothes

23 Beak Street (W1F 9RS) / +44 (0)20 3157 7000 / albamclothing.com
Open daily

Despite being a man, I am a clothes lover, and every time I walk past Albam, just around the corner from Carnaby Street, I am tempted by one of their super-soft Merino knits. Albam is the menswear boutique for modern, well-made wardrobe staples, with a stylish, updated preppy look – think jeans, shirts, chinos, jackets, classic T-shirts and sweaters. Their own-brand clothes are made in partnership with traditional manufacturers, using the finest English and Italian fabrics that actually improve with age. They also carry some other brands that they call friends. So fellas, if you pluck up the courage to join those who like shopping, head over here and you'll find all your simple yet stylish basics – which may well keep you away from the shops for a good while to come.

ALGERIAN COFFEE STORES

Beans and leaves importing pioneers

52 Old Compton Street (W1D 4PB) / +44 (0)20 7437 2480
algcoffee.co.uk / Closed Sunday

Over 100 years since they first opened the shop in Soho, Algerian Coffee
Stores is still one of the leading suppliers for coffee and tea in town, nay
the world. When visiting this place you are truly spoilt for choice, with 80
different types of coffee and 120 teas, and the list continuing to grow as
small, specialty suppliers from more corners of the world are added. They
also have a delicious selection of confectionery, such as pistachio Turkish
delight, and I can't resist the Granny's Secret quince jam. Although the
shop has been updated over the century, it still has lovely original features,
including the wooden counter. This is one of Soho's timeless treasures, but in
case all that isn't enough to persuade you: an espresso is only one pound.

BEYOND RETRO

Shopping for the style conscious

58–59 Great Marlborough Street (W1F 7JY) / +44 (0)20 7434 1406
beyondretro.com / Open daily

Walking through the neon-pink entrance into Beyond Retro, between Carnaby Street and the seedy pavements of Soho proper, is like stepping into a fashion time-warp. This place screams goodies! The friendly assistants double as walking mannequins of vintage style, and the racks are stocked with gems from the 1920s through to the '90s. Everything is here, from '50s silk chiffon dresses to the perfect pair of open-toed heels to go with them, to a complementary clutch and even an outfit for the chap alongside you. My suggestion is to come armed with plenty of time to decide what you want to take back to the future.

HAWKSMOOR SEVEN DIALS

Steak your life on it

11 Langley Street (WC2H 9JG) / +44 (0)20 7420 9390
thehawksmoor.com / Open daily

This classy steakhouse is known for dishing up some of the best hunks of beef in town. Despite the high quality of the food, though, there is nothing pretentious about the atmosphere. It's relaxed and comfortable, and welcomes anybody who simply wants to enjoy some good grub. Although famous for their steaks (which, might I add, are top notch), I feel I must pay homage to their burgers: premium beef seared with chopped bone marrow, an extensive array of toppings including British cheeses and served in brioche buns made by Miller's Bakery in Wimbledon. The shrimps on toast always hits the spot to start things off, and with the dessert menu offering such delights as the classic sticky toffee pudding or a chocolate and salted caramel tart, you can't help but make it a three-course meal.

HOPE AND GREENWOOD

Tempting British confectionery

1 Russell Street (WC2B 5JD) / +44 (0)20 7240 3314
hopeandgreenwood.co.uk / Open daily

I am a self-confessed sucker for sweets: candies, jellies, fudge, sherbet, you name it! Just a short visit to Hope and Greenwood will make you feel like a child again, and a very happy child at that. This little shop, not far from the Covent Garden Piazza, is jam-packed with treats of all sorts, from truffles and licorice to their own scrumptious inventions. I love their selection of fudge including the taste of England that is the all-butter clotted-cream fudge, and personally I must call attention to the peanut butter one, in particular. They'll also put together hampers of goodies, which I can safely say make very well-received gifts. This is British confectionery at its tastiest.

JAMES SMITH & SONS

Umbrellas for all weathers

Hazelwood House, 53 New Oxford Street (WC1A 1BL)
+44 (0)20 7836 4731 / james-smith.co.uk / Closed Sunday

Buses now rumble past where horse-drawn carriages once did when this treasure of the West End was established, back in 1830. Still a family-run business, it exudes the charm of 200-year-old reliable service and has long had a reputation for the highest quality umbrellas. With a large selection of men's, women's and children's, and with the help of the attentive and knowledgeable sales assistants, you can't not find precisely what you are looking for in umbrella form. Just to behold the magnificent rows of walking sticks, parasols and brollies is worth the trip, but let's face it, when in London, you might be in need of an umbrella, right?

LIBERTY

Mock Tudor temple of haberdashery and more

**Regent Street (W1B 5AH) / +44 (0)20 7734 1234 / liberty.co.uk
Open daily**

Since 1875 this London institution has offered eclectic design in the form of fashions, accessories, homewares and haberdashery. It's the type of place my grandmother bought paisley scarves or washbags from. Her mother might have bought a piece of Arts and Crafts furniture and certainly fabrics for dresses and furnishings. Today, it's a showcase of independent jewelry designers (my pick of which being Arman Sarkisyan), clothing (though more so for women than men) and the same famous fabrics. Come the festive season, it has one of the very nicest Christmas decorations departments in town. I can think of no better way to describe this department store extraordinaire than as Oscar Wilde said: "Liberty is the chosen resort of the artistic shopper".

MILDREDS

A veggie's delight

**45 Lexington Street (W1F 9AN) / +44 (0)20 7494 1634 / mildreds.co.uk
Closed Sunday**

As many restaurants as there are in London, it's not easy finding a good all-vegetarian place. When I was in panic over having my veggie friend from France come to stay, Mildreds was recommended to me, thank goodness. I am a true omnivore, but the food at this popular, friendly place was so delicious I forgot about meat for a good few hours. While you are waiting for a table you can enjoy an appetizing cocktail at the bar – perhaps a Wild Hibiscus Royale? For dinner, I enjoyed the Sri Lankan sweet potato and cashew-nut curry, closely and gloriously followed by the chocolate and peanut butter brownie, all of which actually got me asking the question "who needs meat?".

POLPO

Bacaro-style dining

6 Maiden Lane (WC2E 7NA) / +44 (0)20 7836 8448 / polpo.co.uk
Open daily

Understated, relaxed, humble but truly yummy is my way of describing this Venetian restaurant. A little like visiting Polpo's home city, each time I come here, I fall in love with the food more and more. In an urban, bare-bricked space, the dishes are simple but concentrate on using top quality ingredients to make their combinations wonderfully tasty. The spicy pork and fennel meatballs is the perfect thing to tuck into beside a glass of Veneto wine, as is their fried ox tongue and balsamic, or a plate of cicchetti as you'd find on offer in Venice's bacari. The presentation is vibrant, and for ostensibly small plates, the portions are generous, which is always a good thing in my book!

SISTER RAY

Damn good music store

34-35 Berwick Street (W1F 8 RP) / +44 (0)20 7734 3297
sisterray.co.uk / Open daily

A copy of *London Calling*, on vinyl, in perfect condition: my find the last time I visited Sister Ray, and "over the moon" would be an understatement. Although there is an extensive choice of record shops in Soho, none beats this one, in my opinion – and it's the longest-serving independent music store in town. With a huge range of genres, including jazz, rock, house, indie, reggae, and more, good new releases and rare second-hand, there is also a fine selection of exclusive and limited edition stuff. The staff will help you out whatever your musical passion, and if it's not in stock they'll search elsewhere for you, too. When it comes to music, I always go back to Sister Ray. It's a special place.

SOCIAL EATING HOUSE

A celebrated chef's most accessible eatery

58 Poland Street (W1F 7NR) / +44 (0)20 7993 3251
socialeatinghouse.com / Open daily

As the name suggests, Social Eating House is an excellent spot for casual dining. Upscale yet low key, it is but one in the portfolio of super chef Jason Atherton's London restaurants – and probably the most affordable option to taste why so many folks go ga-ga for his grub. The prix fixe lunch yields particularly good value and presents a fantastic chance to sample exquisite dishes such as roasted Cornish cod with Aura potato, romesco, Padrón peppers and ink oil, followed by delectable desserts including vin santo ice cream. Service here is phenomenal, to boot: prompt, friendly and incredibly attentive.

TEA PALACE

Cuppa anyone?

**12 Covent Garden Market (WC2E 8RF) / +44 (0)20 7836 6997
teapalace.co.uk / Open daily**

Everyone knows that Brits love their tea, we are world famous for it. If you're looking to jump on the band wagon, then this is the perfect spot to begin. Tea Palace provides over 120 types, from the classic Builder's Brew, to more alternative tastes, such as Smooth Caramel (which is luscious). Downstairs you'll find their extensive range of teas – black, green, oolong, white, herbal and more – each one in a little bottle allowing you to sample the aromas. In the likely event you want to take some home, you can also enjoy the fact that your teas will be put into cute little tins and labeled specially for you. And if you really are a novice you can also find here all the tea-drinking equipment you'll need, including some beautifully classic teapots. This really is tea in all its glory.

THE BREAKFAST CLUB

International café for brekkie, lunch or supper

33 D'Arblay Street (W1F 8EU) / +44 (0)20 7434 2571
thebreakfastclubcafes.com / Open daily

After hearing many people mention this funky spot, I had to go and see
what the fuss was about. Named in honor of the archetypal '80s film, this
cool, eclectic café in the heart of Soho also happens to be very good at
breakfasts. Their Full Monty is an English Breakfast at its fullest and finest
but there are also favorite ways to start the day from across the globe –
American pancakes with berries, huevos rancheros, falafel wraps, to name
but a few. The apple and cinnamon French toast is delish, and you can throw
in some Bircher museli or a fruitful smoothie to increase the health factor.
Now one of several branches in London, this little egg-yolk-yellow place on
D'Arblay Street was the original, and remains cluttered with the colorful
'80s-childhood memorabilia of the owners that was the initial inspiration.

W. SITCH & CO.

There shall be light

48 Berwick Street (W1F 8JD) / +44 (0)20 7437 3776 / wsitch.co.uk
Closed Saturday afternoon and Sunday

For 11 generations, since 1776, this family-run business has specialized in traditional antique lighting, and they have been doing it rather well. W. Sitch & Co. handle everything from repairs and restoration to reproduction, to make sure old lighting can be used in the modern day. The shop itself seems tiny, in the ground-floor room with walls covered in all sorts of lights and fixtures, but there are four more floors of this Soho townhouse (the relatively new home of the company, since 1903) crammed with light-fittings of various ages and in various stages of readiness to shine again. This place is fascinating, not least for the fact that these guys have provided light since long before the times of electricity and a flick of a switch.

farringdon

holborn, clerkenwell, finsbury

Design geeks, foodies and history buffs listen up! There's
Farringdon and Clerkenwell to explore. This is where, in 1305,
Scottsman William Wallace was drawn and quartered to a
roaring crowd gathered at Smithfield Market, the city's ancient
meat market. Today a memorial commemorates the bloody
occasion. The market is still in operation, with a plethora of
globally renowned restaurants, local gem eateries and a few
of London's oldest pubs filling the warren of streets nearby.
It's not just a gourmand ground zero though. Spend enough
time ambling around the area and you'll become inured to the
litany of slinky models passing between Clerkenwell's handful
of fashion houses. But far outnumbering the models are the
"media types", craftspeople and designers welcoming visitors
into their studios and showrooms. Serving as a buffer between
this zone of creativity and the West End is Holborn, which
somehow manages to remain relatively sedate despite its
location between these popular spots for going out.

1 Caravan
2 Morito
3 Murat Du Carta
4 The Silver Vaults
5 Ye Olde Cheshire Cheese
6 Ye Olde Mitre

CARAVAN

Top coffee spot

11-13 Exmouth Market (EC1R 4QD) / +44 (0)20 7833 8115
caravanonexmouth.co.uk / Open daily

My chosen time to go to Caravan is on those lazy Sundays for a late brunch with a couple of friends, when the poached rhubarb with coconut bread is a delight, or the sardines on toast with slices of avocado. They have some expert baristas serving up some freakishly good coffees, and with the beans being roasted on site, there's a heavenly smell when you first walk in. But you can hang out at this cooly urban place, with King's Cross's local trendies, for breakfast, lunch, drinks and dinner, too. Seasonal ingredients are used to conjure up globally influenced dishes and there's a cool little bar with an extensive range of drinks.

MORITO

New tapas

**32 Exmouth Market (EC1R 4QE)   +44 (0)20 7278 7007   morito.co.uk
Closed for dinner Sunday**

If you have never heard of the legendary Spanish/North African restaurant Moro, your foodie radar might need some adjusting. You'd be forgiven, though, if its younger tapas-bar sibling, Morito, were new to you, as it's less iconic, although catching up fast. In the true Spanish sense, this place is so laid-back, it's almost horizontal. I could easily spend all day here — in fact, a friend and I spent a solid few hours here drinking, chatting and eating mouthwatering dishes such as the puntillitas (crispy baby squid). Morito absolutely has the feel of a tapas joint in Barcelona, but it serves "nuevo tapas" that have a bit of an international twist. The only real difference from being in Spain is that you don't have to wait until bedtime to eat dinner.

MURAT DU CARTA

Quality extra virgin olive oil

76 Compton Street (EC1V 0BN) / +44 (0)20 7251 4721
mroliveoil.com / Closed Sunday

An unlikely grocery vendor, Mehmet Murat (who is of Turkish Cypriot decent) is an electrician by trade. From his electrical supply shop in Clerkenwell, however, he sells his own olive oils side by side with his stock of nuts, bolts and general electrical supplies. His flavorful oils are produced from olive groves he inherited from his parents in central Cyprus, and they deliver the true taste of the Mediterranean, in all its green, peppery richness. Mehmet always welcomes you to sample his aromatic oils with no pressure to buy anything, but with all those sunny flavors titillating your taste buds you'll find it hard to leave empty handed.

THE SILVER VAULTS

Treasure trove beneath the streets

53-64 Chancery Lane (WC2A 1QS)   +44 (0)20 7242 3844
thesilvervaults.com | Closed Saturday afternoon and Sunday

In 1876 The Chancery Lane Safe Deposit Company hit on the idea of renting their subterranean vaults to wealthy Londoners who wanted to safeguard their valuables. Within a few years, these affluent types were increasingly replaced by local silver traders, who were after an equally safe place to keep their stock. After being bombed during the Second World War, the vaults were rebuilt as retail units, where those silver traders sold from their previous storage space. And this is how it remains to this day. It's quite odd descending the stairs and stepping through an enormous vault door but it opens on to a warren of some 30 shops, each filled to the brim with shiny goods. If in search of a rather special souvenir or gift, this is certainly the place for silver – be it antique or new; English, Indian or Japanese; jewelry, a picture frame, a teaspoon or a full dinner service.

YE OLDE CHESHIRE CHEESE

Steeped in pub history

**145 Fleet Street (EC4A 2BU) / +44 (0)20 7353 6170 / No website
Closed Sunday**

In amongst the busy offices and court buildings, this part of town has some true gems of historic pubs, and you can't visit London without sampling a boozer or few. Although the current building of Ye Olde Cheshire Cheese was constructed shortly after the Great Fire of London (1666), food and drink have been served on this site since 1538, and the vaulted cellars possibly belonged to a 13th-century monastery. The unassuming entrance is down an alleyway and once inside you'll discover a maze of many dimly lit rooms. Twain, Tennyson and (Dr Samuel) Johnson were all "regulars" here, as was Dickens and it's said that he makes reference to the pub in *The Tale of Two Cities*. Wheat beer is what to order, and as you sup it you can ponder on how many travelers have been before you to raise a glass in that very spot.

YE OLDE MITRE

King, Church and countrymen

1 Ely Court, Ely Place (EC1N 6SJ) / +44 (0)20 7405 4751
yeoldemitreholborn.co.uk / Closed Saturday and Sunday

Ok, so there's a story here: this pub was originally in Cambridgeshire. No, it wasn't moved here brick by brick, but the land it is built on actually belonged to the Bishop of Ely (he of the eponymous mitre) and as such the street was officially in Cambridgeshire, not London. It dates from 1546 (though rebuilt in 1783), and beside the bar you'll find the preserved trunk of a cherry tree that, it's said, Queen Elizabeth I danced the maypole around. That's once you've found the pub, hidden as it is down the tiniest of alleyways (look out for the sign of a bishop's hat) and few passersby know of its existence. When you've made it, though, what should you order to accompany your real ale? Toasted sandwiches, or a great Scotch egg and mustard.

FLOWERS
82 Kingsland Road (E2 8DP), +44 (0)20 7920 7777
flowersgallery.com, closed Sunday and Monday

HALCYON GALLERY
144-146 New Bond Street (W1S 1SN), +44 (0)20 7100 7144
halcyongallery.com, open daily

HAUSER & WIRTH
23 Savile Row (W1S 2ET), +44 (0)20 7287 2300, hauserwirth.com

LAZARIDES RATHBONE
11 Rathbone Place (W1T 1HR), +44 (0)20 7636 5443, lazinc.com
closed Sunday and Monday

LISSON GALLERY
52-54 Bell Street (NW1 5DA), +44 (0)20 7724 2739
lissongallery.com, closed Sunday

STOLENSPACE
17 Osborn Street (E1 6TD), +44 (0)20 7247 2684, stolenspace.com
closed Monday

WHITE CUBE
144-152 Bermondsey Street (SE1 3TQ), +44 (0)20 7930 5373,
whitecube.com, closed Monday

HALCYON GALLERY

art galleries

A world class scene that defines and defies trends

London's gallery scene is one the world's most engaging. You'll find a diverse variety of works by local talent alongside international up-and-comers and well-established big names.

Ai Weiwei, Tony Cragg, Anish Kapoor – when these heavy hitters aren't working on museum pieces, they're showing works at **Lisson Gallery** in Marylebone, whose portfolio of exhibiting artists reads like a who's who of contemporary art. Large enough for a Louise Bourgeois spider and then some, **Hauser & Wirth** in Mayfair puts on shows of equally celebrated status, while just around the corner at **Halcyon Gallery** even casual passersby often get the chance to ogle iconic pieces by the likes of Warhol.

Just off Oxford Street down a tight but tidy lane, **Lazarides Rathbone** presents edgy works from famous street artists, such as Banksy, Faile, Invader, Ron English and David Choe. For similar global graffiti reach, balanced with the pick of London's own talent, head east to Whitechapel for a browse at **StolenSpace**.

While east, do yourself a favor and see what's up at **Flowers** in Hoxton where an impeccable and thought-provoking selection by established and emerging artists has been wowing art lovers since the early 70s. Once the darling of the Hoxton art scene, **White Cube** is now south of the Thames in an expansive and ultra modern gallery situated on trendy little Bermondsey Street. Recent shows here have included exhibitions by Damien Hirst, Chuck Close and Gary Hume.

southwark and bermondsey

peckham

Even before the arrival of the instantly iconic Shard, this riverside sliver of South London had moved well beyond any up-and-coming phase of development. With some of the city's biggest attractions such as Tate Modern and Shakespeare's Globe situated along the Thames, the area's certainly been a hit with out-of-towners for decades. One particularly popular spot is age-old Borough Market, which can be a tediously touch-and-go endeavor to pass through, as the crowds there never seem to diminish. Nevertheless, prowling around for curbside dining usually proves a thrill for even the most ardent of food snobs. More frequented by local urban foragers but often just as heaving is Maltby Street Market, a short walk away towards Tower Bridge. For a chic stroll through an indie retail haven, a visit to quaint and quirky Bermondsey High Street is a must.

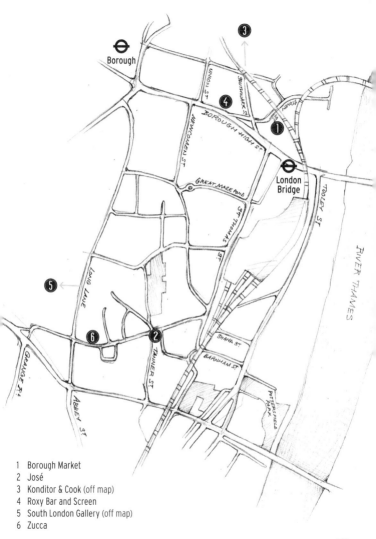

1 Borough Market
2 José
3 Konditor & Cook (off map)
4 Roxy Bar and Screen
5 South London Gallery (off map)
6 Zucca

BOROUGH MARKET

London's most renowned food market

8 Southwark Street (SE1 1TL) / +44 (0)20 7407 1002
boroughmarket.org.uk / Full market Wednesday to Saturday

For anyone who loves good quality produce, buzzing Borough Market is the place: it's as simple as that. Nestled beside Southwark Cathedral, not far from the river, a market has been located around here for 700 years, and on this very land since 1755. Still the local market of the Borough and Southwark community, it now hosts over 100 stalls, including bakers, brewers, butchers, charcuterers, cheese mongers, fish mongers and spice traders. It's all these merchants – many of whom themselves bake, grow or rear what they sell – who make the market so special, sharing a real love for their food and ensuring high standards of taste, provenance and quality. For breakfast, lunch or shopping, or for all three, follow your nose around this vibrant, friendly market and you won't leave hungry.

JOSÉ

Taste-of-Spain tapas bar

104 Bermondsey Street (SE1 3UB) / +44 (0)20 7403 4902
josetapasbar.com / Open daily

José Pizarro, who I might go so far as to call the Godfather of Spanish cuisine, opened up this wonderful tapas and sherry joint in 2011, and it soon became a very popular spot for pinchos-loving folk. The bar is set up perfectly for nibbling and nattering at the same time – sociable dining at its best – and, as always with traditional Spanish cooking, the food has the fun element as well as being delicious. The patatas bravas are mouthwateringly tasty, and another personal favorite of mine is the chorizo ibérico Manuel Maldonado. Wash those down with a Puerto Fino and, believe me, you really can't go wrong.

KONDITOR & COOK

Masterful baking

22 Cornwall Road (SE1 8TW) / +44 (0)20 7633 3333
konditorandcook.com / Open daily

Once upon a time, not so long ago, the majority of coffees served in this city were awful. Save for a handful of bean snob oases, you took your chances when it came to the quality of your cuppa. One of the first safe havens for a worthwhile coffee was Konditor & Cook. These days a decent and well-pulled espresso is a given just about anywhere you may find yourself, thanks in part to the likes of such pioneers. Yet Konditor is considerably more celebrated for its award-winning cakes and pastries, as well as its catering and made-from-scratch cooking. I can vouch that every bite of anything served across the K&C counter (with a smile) is reliably divine, and can certainly brighten up the commute through nearby Waterloo. •

ROXY BAR AND SCREEN

Cozy screening room for a casual night out

128-132 Borough High Street (SE1 1LB) / +44 (0)20 7407 4057
roxybarandscreen.co.uk / Open daily, screenings Sunday to Wednesday

This bar, screening room and live music venue is perhaps the premiere spot for a casual first date in South London (as long as they're not airing a live sports event). Catching a flick, often of the art house or cult classics variety, at the Roxy can be an especially comfy affair with its plush sofas to sink into and a screen large enough and a sound system awesome enough to help you keep in mind that you're not actually watching a movie in the privacy of your own home. Plus grub's reasonably priced. Besides, there are plenty of choices for practically every type of food from street vendors clustered in and around Borough Market to exclusive sky-high dining atop the Shard within relative earshot.

SOUTH LONDON GALLERY

An elegant art space

65-67 Peckham Road (SE5 8UH) / +44 (0)20 7703 6120
southlondongallery.org / Closed Monday

South London Gallery is well known for its contemporary art exhibitions, live art events and its bringing together of established and lesser-known, British and international artists. The stunning building, constructed of Portland stone and handmade pressed bricks, offers a superb gallery space, as well as a café and a garden area. The exhibitions are free and often full of works relating to the local area, modern British art or 20th-century prints, and the general arty "happenings" are either free or very reasonably priced. This is a terrific place to meet friends, eat and drink, and, of course, enjoy some exhibitions.

ZUCCA

Old-school Italian cuisine for contemporary foodies

184 Bermondsey Street (SE1 3TQ) / +44 (0)20 7378 6809
zuccalondon.com / Closed Monday

Situated near the end of one of London's most renowned streets for dining,
Zucca takes the local competition in its stride. With a traditional Italian
kitchen presenting smartly sourced food in a pleasantly contemporary and
spacious setting, it's easy to see how this place maintains its popularity.
Emphasis is on offering a well-balanced and flavorsome expression of
seasonal ingredients and the philosophy is staunchly of the Slow Food
variety. A starter of burrata, wild garlic, capers and chili followed by braised
pig's cheeks with chicory, borlotti, pine nuts and raisins, washed down with
a punchy red? Yes please! But save room for dessert. Even the vanilla ice
cream is a full-on flavor experience. The food might be "slow", but service is
swift, adding up to a gracious dining experience (as long as you've got a rez).

top bookshops

Endless shelves to explore in a city of literary giants

London is as well known for its not always sunny weather as it is for its love of tea. Combine them and you have perfect conditions for curling up with a good book. Luckily, it is also an ideal setting for shopping for that book, with an impressive range of bibliophile stores catering to all tastes, budgets and concerns.

Keen to take home (or perhaps just admire) tomes that are older than many countries? **Jarndyce Antiquarian Booksellers** is the world's leading specialist in 18th- and 19th-century English literature and history. At **Peter Ellis**, don't be surprised if you come across publications from the 16th century or a first edition of *The Memoirs of Sherlock Holmes*. Then there's London's oldest bookshop and "bookseller to the Royal Households" – **Hatchard's** has been selling good reads (including lots of signed titles and special editions) since 1797.

Not quite as ancient but still a gorgeous and historic retail space, Edwardian era **Daunt Books** (pg 82) in Marylebone is a must for lovers of travel literature. For more trip inspiration (and to take a gander at an enviably epic collection of maps) head to **Stanfords**, the largest travel bookshop with also maps, travel accessories and more filling its three-story Covent Garden store.

Offering an equal slice of independent spirit and tempting cake, the **London Review Bookshop** is the eponymous brick-and-mortar extension of Britain's most highly esteemed literary magazine. Just as indie but a lot more design-centric, **Magma** oozes with contemporary eye candy in the way of awesome art and graphic design books, collectable toys, T-shirts and an eclectic mega-load of magazines.

DAUNT BOOKS
83–84 Marylebone High Street (W1U 4QW)
+44 (0)20 7224 2295, dauntbooks.co.uk, open daily

HATCHARD'S
187 Piccadilly (W1J 9LE), +44 (0)20 7439 9921
hatchards.co.uk, open daily

JARNDYCE ANTIQUARIAN BOOKSELLERS
46 Great Russell Street (WC1B 3PA), +44 (0)20 7631 4220
jarndyce.co.uk, closed Saturday and Sunday

LONDON REVIEW BOOKSHOP
14 Bury Place (WC1A 2JL), +44 (0)20 7269 9030
londonreviewbookshop.co.uk, open daily

MAGMA
117–119 Clerkenwell Road (EC1R 5BY), +44 (0) 20 7242 9503
magmabooks.com, closed Sunday

PETER ELLIS
18 Cecil Court (WC2N 4HE), +44 (0)20 7836 8880
peter-ellis.co.uk, closed Sunday

STANFORDS
12–14 Long Acre (WC2E 9LP), +44 (0)20 7836 1321
stanfords.co.uk, open daily

camden and islington

kentish town

Punk's not dead, it's just holed up in Camden along with any number of other subcultures no longer en vogue. Same goes for aging supermodels, who've been known to powder their noses and rub elbows with rock and pop music icons in the local pubs. The daddy of all street markets is in Camden as well, and that seems to be what's drawn all the genre tribes and celebrities to this bustling part of town. Things are more toned down in Islington, where the noteworthy residents tend to be of the political set (Mayor Boris Johnson lives here, for instance). Still, if you want to get down and dirty, the nightlife along Upper Street is among London's more lively, while its dining scene is one of the most dynamic. Shopaholics and thrift-conscious fashionistas will love Islington's many boutiques.

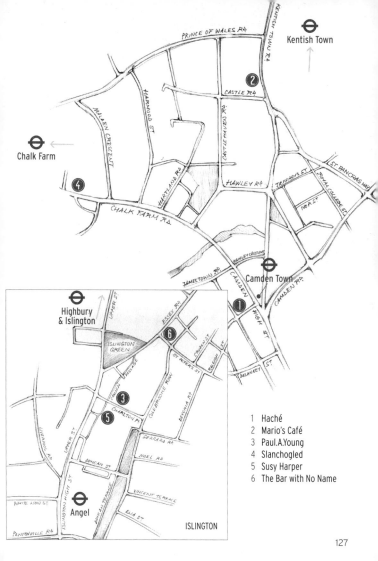

1 Haché
2 Mario's Café
3 Paul.A.Young
4 Slanchogled
5 Susy Harper
6 The Bar with No Name

ISLINGTON

127

HACHÉ

Scrummy burgers

24 Inverness Street (NW1 7HJ) / +44 (0)20 7485 9100
hacheburgers.com / Open daily

I always love the idea of a good burger: a fresh, soft bun, some quality meat and a topping to suit your fancy. But sometimes the reality doesn't meet the hungry expectation. You can be sure, though, this isn't the case at family-run Haché, where the burgers are fantastic and incredibly moreish. The restaurant itself is a narrow space with square tables dotted about, and there's a slightly strange French-meets-English style that just adds to the allure. Try the succulent Steak Bavarian served in a brioche bun; or opt for one of their chicken, lamb or pulled pork burgers.

MARIO'S CAFÉ

Old-school oozing with lost London charm

6 Kelly Street (NW1 8PH) / +44 (0)20 7284 2066 / marioscafe.com
Closed Sunday

A celebrated mainstay among the ever-diminishing number of traditional Italian-owned London caffs, the unassuming Mario's Café exudes a greasy-spoon nostalgia while somehow managing to retain a working class demeanour, and still pull in the gentry punters (who visit without a shred of irony). Sure you can find a better breakfast or lunch in town, but where else are you going to get such a concentrated and distinctively London-y atmosphere to go with your Full English or your plate of homemade Parmigiana? As for the coffee, Mario and co. rack up hipster points by serving beans from East London coffee roasters, Climpson & Sons.

PAUL.A.YOUNG

Handmade chocolates, as inventive as they are delectable

33 Camden Passage (N1 8EA) / +44 (0)20 7424 5750
paulayoung.co.uk / Open daily

With all products made entirely by hand in small batches on the premises and with only fresh ingredients, artisan chocolatier Paul.A.Young and team are responsible for some of the most refined chocolate to be had in London. I'm especially partial to his brownies, hot chocolate and the to-die-for sea salted caramels. But speaking from experience, practically everything in the shop can gain you forgiveness when in the doghouse or is a universally appreciated gift whenever strapped for ideas. This little shop on pretty Camden Passage was the first boutique, and is the perfect, lavishly purple setting to indulge in cocoa splendor.

SLANCHOGLED

Arty farty fun

66 Chalk Farm Road (NW1 8AN) / +44 (0)20 7284 4762
artsandcraftscamden.com / Open daily

If you're the creative type, you'll love this shop. It's the perfect place to take some inspiration and turn it into something real. Holding any arts and crafts material you could ever need, from clay and modeling tools to fabrics and feathers, here is where you can let imagination run riot, and why not turn it into a party with friends? Make some Christmas decorations or some greetings cards, or experiment with mosaics, jewelry or textiles. Or you can take home professional-quality paints and canvases, for some more serious artistic pursuits. Just in case you're wondering, the name means "sunflower" in Bulgarian.

SUSY HARPER

Understated chic designs

35 Camden Passage (N1 8EA) / +44 (0)20 7704 0688
susyharper.co.uk / Open daily

This is a lovely, small, boutique of womenswear and accessories –
Susy Harper being the label of designer Michelle Anslow. The main
emphasis in the clothing, from dresses to trousers to jackets, is on the
textiles and simplicity of form. They are classic but also very stylish
and it's the cut of their pieces that makes them a little different.
Another thing to love about this shop is that they produce their own
prints for the spring and summer seasons, and their fabrics are natural
and ethically sourced.

THE BAR WITH NO NAME

Moody corner joint serving sophisticated cocktails

69 Colebrooke Row (N1 8AA) / +44 (0)7540 528593
69colebrookerow.com / Open daily

I once got into an argument with a friend about how this bar serves some of the best cocktails in London, with neither of us realizing we were both talking about the same exact place. I referred to it as "69 Colebrooke Row" while my compadre called it "The Bar with No Name". Both of us were right though, as this tiny corner bar does indeed offer wise imbibers exceptionally well-crafted drinks, no matter it's title. When you visit, leave any trendy notions about contemporary drinking at the door and let the masterful bartenders in this super dark and swanky little joint mix you something inventive yet classic that's well worth an elbow bend.

CHARLES DICKENS MUSEUM
48 Doughty Street (WC1N 2LX), +44 (0)20 7405 2127
dickensmuseum.com, open daily

FASHION AND TEXTILE MUSEUM
83 Bermondsey Street (SE1 3XF), +44 (0)20 7407 8664
ftmlondon.org, closed Monday

GRANT MUSEUM OF ZOOLOGY
Rockefeller Building, 21 University Street (WC1E 6DE)
+44 (0)20 3108 2052, ucl.ac.uk/museums/zoology, closed Sunday

LEIGHTON HOUSE
12 Holland Park (W14 8LZ), +44 (0)20 7602 3316
rbkc.gov.uk/subsites/museums/leightonhousemuseum1.aspx
closed Tuesday

SIR JOHN SOANE'S MUSEUM
13 Lincoln's Inn Fields (WC2A 3BP), +44 (0)20 7405 2107
soane.org, closed Sunday and Monday

THE GEFFRYE MUSEUM
136 Kingsland Road (E2 8EA), +44 (0)20 7739 9893, geffrye-
museum.org.uk, closed Monday (unless Bank Holiday)

curious museums

Lesser-known collections and homes of notable Londoners

You're not short of choice in London when it comes to museums, but it's well worth making sure some of the less obvious ones are on your list. In Bermondsey, for example, a bright yellow building with a pink door is home to the **Fashion and Textile Museum**. Less a museum and more of a living art space, this is an inspirational venue for fashion lovers, or anyone who appreciates creativity.

For a taste of London-living through the centuries, **The Geffrye Museum** in Hoxton is fascinating to look around. It displays interiors of average homes from the 17th through to the 20th century, with period furnishings packed into the different rooms and lovely gardens too. Or, to see how one particularly famous Londoner lived and worked, head to the **Charles Dickens Museum** in his former house in Bloomsbury.

If display cases full of creepy crawlies and exotic animal bones are more up your street, you shouldn't miss the University of London's **Grant Museum of Zoology** – with everything from saber-toothed tiger canines to rhinoceros skulls, there are 67,000 specimens to see.

Not far from there, in Lincoln's Inn Fields, **Sir John Soane's Museum** shows off his collection of art and architectural drawings and models, just as he left it, packed into his old home. Lit by candlelight at night, this is an atmospheric way to see artworks as they were enjoyed in Georgian times, as well as admire the architect's projects. Another house of an artist that is not to be missed is **Leighton House** (pg 63), exquisitely preserved from the heyday of Victorian Britain.

hoxton and shoreditch

From zero to hero in less than a decade, the western front of the edgy East End is the hip(ster) place to be. But you don't have to be young, bearded and crafty to have a good time around here. With London's financial center melding borders with Shoreditch and a handful of well-connected transportation links dotting the perimeter, there's been a variety of luxury boutiques, high-end eateries and upscale hotels filling the area's post-industrial voids and finding great success in doing so. Meanwhile, an old guard of geezer pubs, curry houses and all sorts of insalubrious venues and business ventures continue to stand their ground (for the time being anyway), bracing themselves as the most gigantic of London's many waves of gentrification crashes heavily and consistently to leave a deluge of new wealth stretching farther and farther eastward beyond the perennially trendy haven of Hoxton Square and its immediate environs.

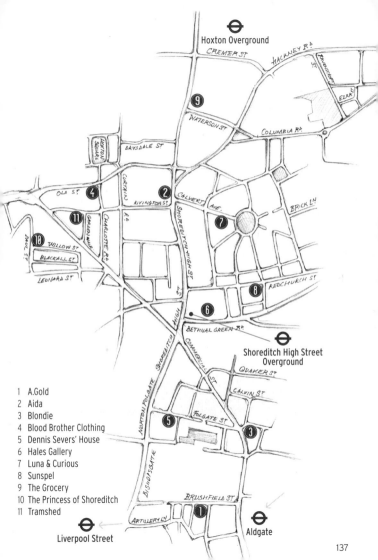

1 A.Gold
2 Aida
3 Blondie
4 Blood Brother Clothing
5 Dennis Severs' House
6 Hales Gallery
7 Luna & Curious
8 Sunspel
9 The Grocery
10 The Princess of Shoreditch
11 Tramshed

Hoxton Overground

CREMER ST.
HACKNEY RD.
RAVENSCROFT ST.
EZRA ST.
WATERSON ST.
COLUMBIA RD.
HOXTON SQUARE
DAYSDALE ST.
OLD ST.
CURTAIN RD.
RIVINGTON ST.
CALVERT AVE.
BRICK LN.
CHARLOTTE RD.
GREAT EASTERN ST.
SHOREDITCH HIGH ST.
PAUL ST.
WILLOW ST.
BLACKALL ST.
LEONARD ST.
REDCHURCH ST.
BETHNAL GREEN RD.

Shoreditch High Street
Overground

NORTON FOLGATE
SHOREDITCH HIGH ST.
COMMERCIAL ST.
QUAKER ST.
CALVIN ST.
FOLGATE ST.
BISHOPSGATE
BRUSHFIELD ST.
ARTILLERY LY.

Liverpool Street

Aldgate

A.GOLD

The village shop in the city

42 Brushfield Street (E1 6AG) / +44 (0)20 7247 2487 / agoldshop.com
Open daily

This shop makes me feel nostalgia for walking home from school, pennies at the ready to fill my boots with multi-colored sugary treats, or when Mum sent me out to get bread and honey from "the local". A.Gold sells a range of village-shop goodies, including homemade Scotch eggs, traditional sweets, local honey, jams and teas, and are specialists in good old British food. The sandwiches here are famous, and rightly so – Paulo Garcia (co-owner with Philip Cundall) makes the most indulgent of fillings fresh daily and uses them generously. My personal favorite is the beer-roasted chicken with herb and onion stuffing: truly golden!

AIDA

For independent labels and a cuppa

133 Shoreditch High Street (E1 6JE) / +44 (0)20 7739 2811
aidashoreditch.co.uk / Open daily

Aida only opened in 2012 but is already a well-established mandatory stop
for East End trend setters. With a front of shop café considered to be among
the area's nicest, there's women's fashion in the back alongside a unisex
parlor offering everything from a quick "Tweak" to "The Full Vintage Make-
Over", plus a whole floor dedicated to men's apparel downstairs. Indie labels
rule the racks, especially if they're British made, and sit comfortably with
the dainty look and feel of the ground floor ladies "department" as well as
the dark and handsome leather luxury down below. Prices for clothes aren't
outrageous and sometimes surprisingly low.

BLONDIE

Hand-picked vintage clothing and accessories

Unit 2, 114–118 Commercial Street (E1 6NF) / +44 (0)20 7247 0050
absolutevintage.co.uk / Open daily

Smartly curated and seasonally replenished, Blondie features clothing and accessories along the lines of loads of designer bags and lots and lots of shoes and is the "ultimate boutique" of Absolute Vintage – they have another store right around the corner that offers a wider (and more hit-or-miss) selection of vintage goods for men and women. Blondie's just for the girls though, especially girls seeking high end apparel from the top brands of decades past. The shop front is rather plain Jane but it's a bit more distinctive inside with a few antique furnishings sprucing things up. The star of the space, though, is the wisely organized display of what's to buy.

BLOOD BROTHER CLOTHING

Contemporary menswear

10 Charlotte Road (EC2A 3DH) / +44 (0)20 7729 5005
blood-brother.co.uk / Closed Sunday

Blood Brother Clothing is the sort of shop that makes me rejoice at the fact that I am male. It isn't for blend-in, wallflower types; this is statement clothing at its best, demonstrating integrity and individuality. The designs support artistic expression, using film, photography and music as inspiration, and are often thought-provoking. I love their tops and sweatshirts with prints and photos emblazoned on them, and I have taken home a few of their Blood Brother beanies, which are not only seriously cool, but incredibly good head warmers.

DENNIS SEVERS' HOUSE

A time capsule of London's past

18 Folgate Street (E1 6BX) / +44 (0)20 7247 4013
dennissevershouse.co.uk / Open Sunday, select Mondays and evenings

Dennis Severs bought this run-down 18th-century house in 1979, and made the choice not to modernize it but to open it up to the public and display its former life, or lives. It gives people a chance to experience glimpses into the lives of Severs' fictional family of inhabitants, the Jervises, from 1725 through to 1919. There are 10 rooms to explore, arranged as they would have been in different epochs during the Jervises' inhabitancy, and lit by candlelight if you visit in the evening. Severs called it "a collection of atmospheres". The feel, the sounds and the smells are really capturing; immerse yourself in this strange wonderland and understand what life would have been like through the ages.

HALES GALLERY

Innovative and contemporary art

7 Bethnal Green Road (E1 6LA) / +44 (0)20 7033 1938
halesgallery.com / Closed Sunday and Monday

Found in Shoreditch's Tea Building, Hales Gallery is one of my treasured favorites. There is one large exhibition space, always showcasing various artists with their visionary and progressive works. The gallery started in 1992 as an alternative art space, but since then has become a commercial gallery, representing artists including Tomoko Takahashi, Spencer Tunick, Hew Locke and Sebastiaan Bremer. Hales regularly hosts exhibitions that you can see for free and it's a great place to either visit with friends or just to mosey around on your own and enjoy the various pieces.

LUNA & CURIOUS

The weird and wonderful

24-26 Calvert Avenue (E2 7JP) / +44 (0)20 3222 0034
lunaandcurious.com / Open daily

This quirky boutique located in hip Shoreditch offers a stunning selection of clothing and objects. Whenever you browse in Luna & Curious you'll find something different, and that something could be anything from beautiful and wacky jewelry, such as beetle-wing necklaces, to stunning handcrafted ceramics, off-the-wall objects and clothing – a few highlights from my last visit: butter dishes in the shape of bath-tubs, Cherokee-style dip-dyed feather necklaces, handmade butterfly teapots and bird's-feet booties for babies. Everything featured in the shop is about intriguing British design, and they showcase lots of artists' work, many of whom are from around the local area.

SUNSPEL

Handsome everyday clothes to wear for years

7 Redchurch Street (E2 7DJ) / +44 (0)20 7739 9729
sunspel.com / Open daily

A little-known fact is that the millions of boxers-wearing men in the UK might not be doing so if it weren't for this particular shop in Shoreditch – they were first to introduce them, back in 1947. With over 150 years of experience, this is a top-notch label for classic British menswear. Sunspel is famous for their T-shirts, polos and, of course, those boxer shorts, and everything is of the highest quality. Each item of clothing shows true craftsmanship, using traditional techniques and mixing them with new ideas to create their very own innovative yet classic, personal style. In particular, I'm a fan of their gorgeous cashmere scarves and vintage wool jackets. This is an absolute treat for the gents, and there's a ladies store just down the road, too.

THE GROCERY

Good shopping, in all senses

54-56 Kingsland Road (E2 8DP) / +44 (0)20 7729 6855
thegroceryshop.co.uk / Open daily

The Grocery is one of the leading organic food establishments in London, stocking delicious things from all over the world. Do some shopping here and you'll come away with bags of stuff that is super healthy, locally sourced or fairtrade and reasonably priced for all that, too. I'm a bit of a fiend when it comes to their bread, chocolate and juices, and a few bottles of their wine doesn't go amiss either. Once you've done your foraging, make sure to stop by the café tucked away at the back of the shop. It's the perfect place to relax and grab some breakfast or lunch, with some very good coffee and a lovely choice of salads as well.

THE PRINCESS OF SHOREDITCH

270-year-old modern pub

76-78 Paul Street (EC2A 4NE) / **+44 (0)20 7729 9270**
theprincessofshoreditch.com / **Open daily**

The Princess of Shoreditch is the epitome of the new breed of pub:
a traditional old watering-hole with a long history, modernized into a pub-
cum-restaurant that offers the tastefully up-to-date version of exactly what
has happened on this site for centuries. It's thriving by keeping up with the
times, as it has done for 270 years. In the busy bar you can tuck into classics
such as pie and mash, Barnsley chop, beer-battered fish and chips, and sticky
toffee pudding, alongside your drinks. Alternatively, you can head for the
restaurant, up a spiral staircase, and relish cured wild duck breast, slow roasted
pork belly or venison haunch followed by cheeses of a truly English selection:
Stilton, Lancashire Strong Bomb and Stinking Bishop. Yum.

147

TRAMSHED

Steak and chicken, straight up

32 Rivington Street (EC2A 3LX) / +44 (0)20 7749 0478
chickenandsteak.co.uk / Open daily

Wow, what a place. From the outside the building doesn't look like much: plain and understated. Inside, however, is a huge warehouse-type scenario with high ceilings and an impressively large floor-space. Hanging above everyone's heads as they eat and drink is Damien Hirst's famous *Cow and Cockerel* – very fitting, as these guys serve strictly steak and chicken. The owner, Mark Hix, is known for his love of art and decided to create his own gallery downstairs from the restaurant, where exhibitions frequently change, as well as to display works in the eating spaces. Back to the food, though, and the giant Yorkshire pudding with whipped chicken liver is amazing. The salt beef and bobby bean salad also deserves a shout out too.